Collect All 21!

Memoirs of a *Star Wars* Geek - The First 30 Years

Also by John Booth

Crossing Decembers – a novel

Collect All 21!

Memoirs of a *Star Wars* Geek - The First 30 Years

By John Booth

Collect All 21!

Memoirs of a *Star Wars* geek – The First 30 Years

By John Booth

Front cover by Kirk Demarais

Back cover text written by Adam Besenyodi.

First printing, July 2008

Cover revision and foreword added April 2009

ISBN: 978-1-4357-4376-2

For Jenn and Kelsey:
I wouldn't trade you
for a pair of Rocket Firing Boba Fetts.

Foreword

It was 1986. The next *Star Wars* movie – showing what happened after *Return of the Jedi* – was going to be released. For three years, I'd been waiting. *Star Wars* appeared in 1977, *Empire* in 1980, and *Jedi* in 1983. Of course the next movie would appear in 1986.

This was before the Internet. It was hard to find information on movies in (or not in) production. As 1986 drifted on, surely the advertising campaigns and merchandising tie-ins would begin soon.

I had a much longer wait than I'd ever anticipated.

This was what being a *Star Wars* fan in those heady times was like. It was the yearning, the desire for more, that made the little bites of life in a galaxy far, far away all the sweeter.

The memories of those times are something deeply personal, yet also in a sense shared with everyone else who imagined they were Chewbacca, lusted after the newest *Star Wars* playset, and drew crude cartoon pictures of the Death Star blasting a ship into oblivion.

My most vivid *Star Wars* memory is from the first time I saw *Return of the Jedi*. I was in high school, and old enough to see it with friends, without parents. We were of the right generation and incredibly excited. The action exploded onto the screen as we gaped and took it all in. During the climactic final battle, Luke had just given in to his anger and Darth Vader crumpled under his furious rain of blows. A girl in our group was so caught up in the action that she yelled, "Kill him! Kill him!!"

None of us knew Vader would be redeemed in the next five minutes of screen time. He was still the epitome of pure evil. The girl wasn't joking – she was clutching the back of the seat in front of her and desperately willing the hero to victory.

The movie ended and we left, exhilarated by what we'd seen. The wait had been worth it, and it was officially the Best Movie Ever.

Until the next *Star Wars* movie came along in another three years' time, of course.

These are just a couple of my memories. Reading John Booth's memories of the same times brought these, and many more, flooding back. Any *Star Wars* fan of our generation will have their own fond recollections. They are our own, but in them we share a common bond. *Star Wars* is a fabric that weaves the lives of a whole generation together.

And we've been very lucky. We got to relive much of that keen young excitement 20 years later, when many of us had spouses and jobs and kids of our own. We're older and more sophisticated, of course, and it's easy to find flaws in new things, while ignoring those in the things we loved as children. But we never let *Star Wars* die, and the anticipatory excitement we felt was just as real as when we were kids.

Anticipation and imagination are most of the fun of being a fan. Seeing the movies is wonderful, but nothing beats the thrill of waiting in line for an hour, thinking and chatting with friends about what you're going to see, racing for the best seats, settling in to a comfortable position for the next two hours, squirming uncontrollably as the lights dim, the curtains part, those familiar blue words flash on to the screen, and then the crash of the John Williams soundtrack blasts you into another galaxy...

Relive it again now, and see why, after all these years, *Star Wars* still delivers wonderful new memories.

David Morgan-Mar

March 2009

David Morgan-Mar is the creator of the online comics Irregular Webcomic *and* Darths and Droids. *He also writes for the GURPS role-playing game line, has designed computer programming languages for orangutans and evil necromancers, and has a Ph.D. in astrophysics from the University of Sydney. He lives in Australia with a very patient wife.*

Introduction

When I was in my mid-twenties and living in Florida, I was obsessed with the idea that there were still long-lost *Star Wars* toys lying hidden in the house where I grew up in Ohio. On visits home, I'd crawl into the darkness underneath the basement stairs, back into regions far too scary and cobwebbed to have braved as a kid, sweeping my hands along the cement floor, peering by flashlight into the corners. I'd lie on my stomach on the floor and stretch my arms underneath the cabinets where we still kept games like Foto-Football and Battleship and Risk. I'd squeeze back into the corner behind the water heater and poke my fingers into the track that held the sliding access door.

My only successes were finding a tiny blaster – I'm thinking it was Lando Calrissian's – and discovering my old Greedo lying behind the deep freezer, grime-coated and missing his antennae completely.

I looked through the hot, stuffy attic, too, thinking maybe there were some empty boxes or old action figure cardbacks tucked inside bigger cartons. (No *Star Wars* stuff, but I did find our original Atari Video Computer System package up there. Mom was real big on saving boxes.)

Writing this book's been a lot like those searches.

In early 2007, with the 30th anniversary of the original *Star Wars* movie release coming up, I started keeping notes for a project I called in my head "Every *Star Wars* Memory I've Ever Had." I carried notepads everywhere and wrote myself memory-jogging snippets like "Blue Snag Carnegie Library" and "Vader funhouse – William."

I published the first resulting essay, "Where the Fun Begins," on my website, FieldsEdge.com, and, encouraged by a local radio journalist friend, adapted it into a commentary for WKSU, a Northeast Ohio affiliate of National Public Radio. Eleven more essays followed online, and during the writing, I started working toward the goal of collecting them in book form, along with previously unpublished essays, too.

The great thing was, along the way, the more I organized and collected these memories, the more I rediscovered. It was like all those times I've sat down with other *Star Wars* fans and talked about the fun we had as kids growing up absolutely nuts for these movies and toys and characters.

These are some – maybe even most – of the *Star Wars* memories I've been carting around in my head for three-plus decades. It's been fun poking around under the basement stairs in my brain. Consider this book my sharing of the flashlight.

John Booth

Where the Fun Begins:
Summer 1977

I don't remember the first time I saw *Star Wars*.

I remember wanting to see it, and I remember having seen it.

That actual first time, though, that I saw "A long time ago..." glowing blue in the darkness, and heard that slam-you-back-in-your-seat opening score, and read the majestic opening crawl, that's all gone. "Lost" probably isn't the word for it – more likely it's just pulped in somewhere with 30 years' worth of other *Star Wars* memories, and I just haven't looked in the right corner of my brain yet.

I was only six-and-a-half, after all, back in the summer of 1977. (And I'll always believe that was the absolute perfect age to be for a movie like *Star Wars* to come along and sear itself into my head.) How could I know that I was supposed to be committing these all-important moments to memory?

Some of the stuff I do remember about *Star Wars* back in that summer after kindergarten: My first little brother was just an infant, and we had just moved from our house near the Pro Football Hall of Fame in Canton, Ohio, out to what were then the boondocks of Lake Township. There are *Star Wars* memories that can't possibly reflect actual reality. For instance, my friend Ford, from kindergarten, and his older brother had seen it. They'd also seen *Close Encounters of the Third Kind*, and one night their dad was bringing me home from a day at their house, and we were talking about the movies. We were riding in their dad's Jeep, and Ford and his brother were kind of talking about both movies at once, and his brother said, "Yeah, they had these great big heads and skinny bodies," – obviously talking about the *Close Encounters* aliens – and Ford and I were confused because we'd still been talking about *Star Wars*.

Here's the thing, though: *Close Encounters* didn't come out until November of 1977, months and months after *Star Wars*. And I know that night in the Jeep, I hadn't seen *Star Wars* yet, but I'm also absolutely certain I saw it the summer it came out, or at least by fall when I started first grade.

So I can't work that memory out, but it still doesn't make it any less real. Maybe Ford's older brother was talking about a preview or a magazine article or something he'd seen with the *Close Encounters* aliens in it. That still feels more like an after-the-fact justification, though, than what really happened.

I have the feeling, though I can't be sure, that the first time I saw *Star Wars* was at the McKinley Twin movie theater on 30th Street in Canton. Great movie theater – cavernous and deep and boasting both a main level and a balcony. The last movie I remember seeing there was Tim Burton's *Batman* the summer after I graduated from high school. Since then, the McKinley's been converted into a big video rental store.

Still, I can't remember actually seeing *Star Wars* for the first time. Sometimes I wonder what it would be like to have a reverse *Total Recall* done – have *Star Wars* taken out of my head so I could watch it for the first time again. Then I think what a gut punch it would be if I didn't like it.

I do remember sitting on the living room floor at home afterward with a box of crayons and a stack of construction paper and feverishly illustrating a project I cleverly titled "My *Star Wars* Book," which consisted of probably eight or ten pages, each with a single character portrait. I don't have the book anymore, but I do have some drawings from early 1978 (God bless Mom for not only saving them, but labeling them in ballpoint on the back!) that are probably pretty similar. There's C-3PO, and an R2-D2, and my own interpretation of the cover of Marvel Comics' *Star Wars* Issue #5.

I know I struggled with a couple aspects of "My *Star Wars* Book." For starters, I had no black crayon. I know this because while I don't have my drawing of the "Storm Trooper" anymore, I've got a pretty decent mental picture of it, and the poor guy's drawn in white and blue-green. And his helmet's a big blocky square. (Don't ask how I drew Darth Vader without a black crayon. Either I didn't even bother to attempt it, or it came off so poorly I've banished it from memory.) I remember asking Dad how he thought you'd spell "Kenobi," because I was meticulously labeling each drawing. I was also apparently trying to perfect the art of reproducing the *Star Wars* title logo, since it's all over the drawings that survived.

Two of those pictures from 1978 also poke into some foggier memories. One is a pen-and-crayon drawing of a green lightsaber (my light blue crayon must've been MIA, too), the other of a red one. Nobody's holding them, and there's no background. They're just floating there.

And I labeled them "The Good Force" and "The Bad Force."

I guess I can see the whole "energy field created by all living things" bit going well over my head, but I still don't know how exactly I managed to somehow turn "The Force" into the actual lightsabers themselves.

While I can't remember seeing *Star Wars* for the first time, I can remember a few of the other times I caught it on the big screen.

Once was at a drive-in, and the only scene that really sticks in my head is Han's meet-up with Greedo in the cantina. That was the first time Dad saw *Star Wars*, though he'd been hearing me rave about it incessantly, I'm sure. I remember him asking me if I thought he'd be able to understand the plot.

Then I asked him what a plot was.

I'm pretty sure I also saw *Star Wars* at the Belden Twin Cinemas (long since replaced by a series of interchangeable and forgettable strip-mall shops), and at the old Mellett Mall movie theater during one of the re-releases.

I saw it 23 times in the theater. At least, that's the number I settled on decades ago when I was trying to count and lost track.

It's funny – seeing a movie over and over used to mean a lot more than it does now. It required commitment and time and, for me, an adult to drive the car and buy the tickets. In the videotape and subsequent DVD eras, repeated viewings are the norm. And movies once took eons to make the jump to the television screen, so it literally took me years to come close to the two-dozen-viewings mark for *Star Wars*. My daughter had probably seen *Toy Story* twice as many times by her third birthday.

There's no way, after almost 30 years, for me to even estimate how many times I've seen *Star Wars*. And when I say *Star Wars*, I mean *STAR WARS*. As big a fan as I am of the entire film series, even the hyper-flawed but still mostly-fun *Episodes I, II* and *III*, the first movie, in my mind, will always be known by the saga's overarching title. Growing up, even after *The Empire Strikes Back* and *Return of the Jedi* came out, my friends and I never referred to the first one as *A New Hope*. It was always *Star Wars*.

Just like the first time.

Proof of Purchase

Star Wars even made school supplies cool. I still have the 9½-by12½-inch Mead portfolio folder I carried around in second grade. Obi-Wan's on one side, two Stormtroopers on the other, and on one of the inside pockets, there's that rear-three-quarters shot of a Star Destroyer. The Finney's 39-cent price tag is still stuck inside. The folder's in two pieces, and the edges are worn soft as old socks, but when I hold it, I can smell crayons and purple-ink mimeographed worksheets and Elmer's School Glue and brick walls and the cement floors of the second-grade basement hallway at Hartville Elementary, and remember sitting on the carpet in our room listening to Miss Hogan read "James and the Giant Peach."

The Droids We Were Looking For:
How Kenner Took Ownership
of My Childhood

I watched as much television as any other kid in the early 1970s. Probably too much. And for every brain-building show like *Sesame Street*, there was a *Sigmund and the Sea Monsters* or a Road Runner cartoon to even things out.

Either way, the television screen was an impervious and immovable boundary. When the set was turned off, I didn't clear the kitchen table to set up my *Electric Company* "Heyyyy Youuuuu GUUUUUuuuys!" Board Game or beg my parents to get me the cave playset and an extra sleestak to take on Marshall, Will and Holly in some backyard *Land of the Lost* action. (*Land of the Lost* intrigued me to no end. I was really sucked in by the sort-of-scary hissing sleestaks, the mystical hovering pylons, and the power crystals glowing on what looked like cafeteria trays hidden in black-lit caves. I enjoy those memories, which is why I haven't tried to watch the show in years. Did that once when Cartoon Network showed the 1980s animated *Godzilla* production. It sucked so bad I wept for the Saturday morning hours wasted.)

And then came *Star Wars*.

Seeing it in the movie theater made the first, deep and indelible Bantha track, but things really got rolling with the merchandising – the toys and the games and the comics and the books and the bed sheets.

For Pete's sake, bed sheets! What else besides *Star Wars* could have gotten a 7-year-old excited over a set of freaking BED SHEETS?

I still have my Escape from Death Star board game, and a 140-piece puzzle of Han Solo and Chewbacca, either of which could be the first *Star Wars* toy I ever got, since Kenner didn't manage to get action figures out until 1978. (It's almost unfathomable these days to imagine a movie like *Star Wars* being launched with absolutely no toy production plans in place. As I'm writing this, it's late April 2007, and I've already seen stuff in the stores for *Spider-Man 3* and *Shrek the Third*, neither of which will hit theaters until next month. This is, of course, all *Star Wars'* fault, for better or worse.)

The first *Star Wars* figure I owned was R2-D2, with an asterisk in the record book, because I really count Darth Vader as number one. Here's why:

There was a kid down the street, about a year younger than me, named Chris. I don't think his family lived there very long because I only remember him from my first year in the neighborhood, when I was in first grade.

Even though Chris was only in kindergarten, I remember him as kind of a bad kid. Not like stealing or hitting or smoking bad, but he was the first kid I ever heard swear regularly. Among his favorite expressions was "Well, what're we waiting for, Mr. Magoo shit?" His mouth actually got me in trouble once: My dad sat me down one night to tell me that Chris's mom had heard her little angel using naughty words, and that he said I taught them to him. I think Dad was pretty well aware of the true situation, because the talking-to I got seemed more out of obligation than actual concern about me running around with a Richard Pryor vocabulary. The conversation ended with Dad laughing and saying, "No more swearing, dammit."

Chris used to meet me sometimes when I got off the school bus in the afternoons, and sometimes we'd sit on the small stacks of bricks that flanked the drainage ditch in a neighbor's front yard and I'd share leftovers from my lunch. Then we'd walk up the street to my house and maybe have a snack and then play outside for awhile.

Chris was the first kid I knew who ever had *Star Wars* toys. The bus pulled up the street one day and from my seat, I saw him standing by the stop sign clutching a Landspeeder. Sweet God, a Landspeeder right out of the movie, just waiting in his hands there at the little crossroads where our school bus stopped. I dashed up to him, spastic at the sight of the thing, and he completely ignored me. He said hi to Rick, the kid who lived across the street from me, though, and then turned to me and said he was going to play with Rick that day.

I seriously thought I was going to cry, watching them walk up the street. Come on! Rick wasn't even a *Star Wars* fan! What the hell?!

Once, Rick and I camped out in a tent in my backyard. We hadn't invited Chris, but somehow he found out and apparently was at home crying. His older sister came over to my house before we'd settled in the tent for the night and asked if Chris could pleeeeeease sleep out with us? He really, really wanted to, and look, she'd brought us some little baby toads she'd caught in her yard, and we could have them if we'd just let Chris sleep over in the tent, pleasepleasepleeeeease? (Wow. That's a strangely dedicated older sister, no?)

We gave in, though we turned down the baby toad offering. That night, Chris told me that women's boobs were sometimes called headlights, and that his little translucent green toothbrush with silver flecks in its handle was actually a *Star Wars* toothbrush. Really! It used to have stickers of Darth Vader and Grand Moff Tarkin on the handle, but they'd worn off, for real!

Chris did eventually share his *Star Wars* toys with me, and I convinced him to trade me his R2-D2 figure for something, but I don't remember what. His initials were written in black marker on the bottom of Artoo's feet. I treasured that figure. Didn't put it down, clicked the dome head back and forth, made him stroll over boundless carpetscapes and probably even hid it under my pillow that night. I didn't tell my parents about it, because I didn't want to be the kind of kid who ripped off littler kids, even though we'd made a trade and it wasn't an outright con.

It was a glorious time span of less than 24 hours. The next day, Chris told me his mom had ordered him to trade back for the figure. How'd she find out? Oh, well, see, she had put a little spring in his pants pocket, Chris explained, so that he couldn't hide things in there, and when he came home the day before, and there was no R2-D2 sticking out of his pocket, his mom had obviously known that he'd given it away, and she'd gotten reeeeallly mad, so he just *had* to trade it back.

And so my *Star Wars* action figure count dropped back to zero.

There was an upside, though: It wasn't too long before my parents did actually manage to buy me all 12 of the original figures, and because I'd collected the whole dozen, I used their proofs-of-purchase to buy a mail-away display stand advertised on the cardbacks. I still have it – the backdrop fell apart years ago, and the stand is cracked in a few places, and the label on the front is partially torn off, but I'll never get rid of it.

Before the figures came, though, I got a Landspeeder of my own.

I don't remember where I got it or why, but sending it zipping through our kitchen on its spring-loaded, "floating ride" set of wheels was a sheer plastic-driven rush. I'd shove it careening against the baseboards and try to make a head-on hit that would pop open the engine compartment cover. I'd flip the wheel-activation lever so the speeder would rest flat and lie still, like a wolf waiting to leap at prey, and then I'd flick the switch that engaged the wheels and I could imagine the jet-engine scream of the Landspeeder turbines rocketing it across the desert flats.

Within a day or two, the thrill was gone. Not in a bored-with-it sense, but in a John-lost-his-favorite-toy-ever sense.

I'd been playing outside in the front yard with some of the other neighborhood kids, including Melanie, the girl from down the street, and I thought it would be fun to pick up our cat, Tabby, and put her on Mel's back.

Tabby was an outdoor cat, so she had her claws, and she sank them into Mel's back like she was clinging to a maple trunk. Mel screamed, and Tabby's claws raked down her back. The cat ran off, and Mel kept crying. I felt horrible.

After making sure Mel got home okay, my parents lectured me something fierce and then asked me to pick a punishment, something they'd never done in my seven years of existence. (They also offered me the chance to get a spanking. Like I was going to choose that.) I tried the "no dessert for a month" bit. Denied: We didn't have dessert regularly anyway. I'm sure my parents probably put forth some sort of television restriction, but please, why not just ask me to stop breathing?

Then I thought of the Landspeeder. I offered to give it up for a week. They said make it a month, and we had a deal. They packed it back in its glorious full-color packaging and set it on top of the refrigerator, where I could see it constantly, that kid on the side of the box mocking me.

When the calendar changed, I asked for it back. No dice, my parents said, it's only been a couple weeks. Punishment started mid-month. I'd known that, but I figured it was worth a try.

Eventually, when I got it back, my Landspeeder needed a driver.

Time to get my first *Star Wars* figure.

We went to the Hobby Center store at the mall, Belden Village. The figures were $1.75 apiece, and the display towered over me. I pretty quickly narrowed my choices down to Luke Skywalker and Darth Vader, but that deadlock lasted awhile.

I made the case for Luke: It's his Landspeeder, for starters. And he is the hero, since he blew up the Death Star and rescued Princess Leia and all, even if he's not as cool as Han Solo or his ship.

But then there's the pro-Vader side: Come on. He's Darth Freaking Vader. Luke's a farm kid in a dirty shirt, this guy's a towering mass of black metal who can crush your throat single-handed or no-handed, and besides, the Luke figure is almost just like a miniature Ken doll or something, whereas the Vader figure is cool and sci-fi and looks like no other action figure in the world.

I picked Vader. Had him tooling around in the Landspeeder, imagining he was cruising around on the surface of the Death Star. Ridiculous? Not to a 7-year-old. I mean, physics aside, Vader's in that suit, and he could probably do a cannonball into the sun for all I knew. I remember telling my parents that Vader was just "more exciting."

After that, I don't remember the specifics by which my collection – though we didn't call them collections then, they were just our *Star Wars* toys – grew. I got the Land of the Jawas, and still have it, though the cardboard Sandcrawler backdrop is long gone. (Even though it looked cool, the tiny elevator was a pain to work smoothly, to say nothing of trying to fit figures onto the microscopic pegs sandwiched inside the thing.) The escape pod the set came with was pretty neat, though, and I loved the system of footpegs, levers and spring plates by which I could carefully set up the Jawas' ambush of R2-D2. I got an X-Wing – again, still have it, even though all four laser guns, three of the wings and the plastic cockpit window are missing. And a TIE Fighter with the pop-off wings, too. Great not only for simulating battle damage, but for rigging any manner of catapulting experiments.

I never got the Millennium Falcon, but the Christmas of 1978 I got the best toy ever: The Kenner Death Star Playset. A better non-electronic toy was never made, and even the original Atari Video Computer System I got a few years later only barely edges it on my all-time favorite list.

Years later, when I started seeing Death Stars for sale in their original boxes, I was surprised to see how small the package was, because I remembered the toy as being huge. But then, thinking about it more, I realized that the thing came in about a hundred pieces.

And it was worth every painstakingly-applied decal.

Four full levels, a working elevator, an exploding laser cannon, a trapdoor, a trash compactor with foam-rubber garbage chunks that mashed the figures ever so nicely and popped open an exit hatch at the last minute. The set even seemed to fill in details that were either unseen in the movie or glimpsed just barely, like that giant laser cannon, the interior monitor screens showing the climactic dogfight, the bridge across the chasm that Luke and Leia could've used if he hadn't blasted the control panel, and the mysterious trash compactor monster, the Dianoga, whose name I didn't know until a few years later when I read *The Jedi Master's Quizbook*. (In the movie, you only saw an eye and a few tentacles, but the toy version of the monster had a bizarre *Jaws*-inspired mouth that was nothing like I would have pictured.)

And the detail of incorporating a narrow ledge and the tractor beam controls at the top of the elevator shaft? Absolute genius.

I remember playing with it the day I got it, trying to get Dad to snap a picture of me just as I "blew up" the cannon on the top level.

With so many pieces, I know it probably didn't take long for my Death Star to start falling into disrepair. By the time I was in middle school, I think the only parts left were the elevator shaft, the trash compactor and monster, and the body of the laser cannon, though without its long extended muzzle.

The only problem with the Death Star was that it was a strictly stay-at-home toy. Ships and action figures you could take over to your friends' houses, but not that thing.

In first grade, Mike D. was the first friend I ever had who didn't live in our neighborhood. Sometimes our parents would send notes to school and let us ride the bus to each other's house. Mike was the only other kid I knew who was really as into *Star Wars* as I was. I was insanely jealous because his dad had brought him some *Star Wars* trading cards back from a trip to Germany, and they were these cool glossy things, like playing cards, and they came in a pack of 50 or 60, not like the flimsy cardboard Topps cards I collected in packs of less than a dozen.

Mike, who would grow up to be an artist, also had the *Star Wars* Portfolio, that collection of Ralph McQuarrie pre-production paintings, which I thought were just amazing. Once, we spent a few hours sitting and tracing bits and pieces of each painting to create our own custom *Star Wars* pictures. When we were older, he gave me that portfolio. You can still see our pencil-point indentations on some of the prints.

Mike's parents had a stereo with a record player, and they'd gotten him the 45 rpm single of the *Star Wars* theme (disco rendition), which we thought was particularly awesome because it included laser sound effects. The flip side was the Cantina band theme, similarly rendered. His mom had some friends over once, and while they were sitting in the family room, we put the Cantina music on and paraded through the house playing invisible alien saxophones.

We didn't play much with action figures over at Mike's house. I remember running around inside and outside and pretending we were tearing through the Death Star and blasting Stormtroopers and confronting Darth himself. And I know Mike had the small-scale die-cast X-Wing, because I remember careening around the big wraparound porch at his house, weaving in and out of the pillars with that ship in my hand while he flew my die-cast Millennium Falcon.

That Falcon was the only one of the little metal Kenner ships I had. Dad was going to Click's one day – this was the closest grocery and department store, and it was technically called "Click" or "Acme Click," but nobody ever said they were going to Click, because it just sounded funny. Maybe that's why now it's called Acme Fresh Market and has nothing but groceries. I took fifty cents of my own money with me, even though I knew fifty cents wouldn't get you squat in the Kenner/*Star Wars* world.

What I found was the die-cast Falcon. I'd never seen it before, except in a weird white-and-red prototype form that Kenner put in one of the toy catalogs they included with other *Star Wars* toys. The one sitting on the shelf in front of me, though, was gorgeous and detailed and featured not only retractable landing gear, but a rotating laser cannon and radar dish!

I picked it off the shelf, took it to Dad.

He was skeptical. "How much is that?" he asked.

"Um...five," was all I said.

"Do you have five dollars?"

"NobutIhavefiftycentswithmeandIcanpayyoubacktherestandI'll doextrachorespleasePleasePlease."

At a buck a week allowance, this was like signing a mortgage.

But seriously: We're talking about the Millennium Falcon here.

I still have that one, too, only it's been missing the plastic radar dish for decades. I call it my limited edition post-*Return of the Jedi* version.

When Mike and I were in high school and hadn't been close for a number of years, we kind of renewed our friendship over a couple afternoons in the computer art department. Fiddling with the video cameras and the nifty new Apple Macintoshes, Mike figured out that you could also hook the video cable to a VCR, and we captured a bunch of *Star Wars* screengrabs off a video tape of the trilogy I'd recorded from cable TV showings.

Sitting there, watching *Star Wars* frame by frame, pausing and rewinding and talking, for a little while, it was almost 1978 again.

Minus the invisible alien saxophones.

Proof of Purchase

Mom got me a *Star Wars* cake for my eighth birthday. This was 1978, mind you, so this wasn't a photo-icing cake or even a cartoon-style airbrushed cake: This was a "Cake Lady in Canton, could you do please do something for my son who's gonzo for this movie" cake.

This was plain white icing sheet cake and line-piped bootleg-looking drawings of a Jawa and R2-D2 and Vader and a TIE Fighter, with a bright yellow lightsaber in the middle and Happy Birthday Johnny in orange and white letters.

And I loved it. It was the coolest looking cake I would get until my high school graduation, when Mom had my best friend Aaron draw a cartoon of me driving a Corvette, which she had the Cake Lady in Canton render in icing, and even that one's a close call.

My brother Nick got a *Return of the Jedi* cake when he was ten: Vader and Luke dueling against the deep blue backdrop of the Throne Room window outlined in fat white icing lines. It's a little more detailed than mine was, and by this time they were able to color in backgrounds and stuff.

I was 16 by then.

I was still a little bit jealous.

Into A Larger World:
Star Wars Jumps off the Screen

For either my eighth birthday or Christmas 1978, I don't remember which, my Aunt Carol gave me three books, wrapped together in plastic. Their spines read "*Star Wars*" and "The Marvel Comics Illustrated version of *Star Wars*" and some weird-sounding title I'd never heard of that made me think, "What does she think I am, a novelist?" because I thought "novelist" mean someone who read a lot of books with small print and no pictures.

That third book was "Splinter of the Mind's Eye" by Alan Dean Foster, and when I actually took off the shrink-wrap and realized that I was holding a previously-untold *Star Wars* story, I was just bowled over. I still re-read it every few years and find that my mind creates the same mental pictures as when I was little. ("Splinter" was adapted into a comic book in the 1990s, and I never read it, in part because the illustrations clashed so violently with those in my own imagination that I decided after seeing just a page or two that I'd rather keep my 8-year-old interpretation intact.)

A couple things in "Splinter" have always stood out in my head: The gross-out scenes, like the one where a prisoner has an eye put out by an Imperial officer, and the description of a post-fight combatant as he "chucked the double handful" of an enemy's remains on the ground, where it lay "moist and glistening"; Luke, pinned face-down on a pond floor in a hand-to-hand battle as he feels "the clean grains [of sand] pressing into his nostrils."

When the *Return of the Jedi* Sketchbook came out about five or six years later, I was surprised to see references to "Yuzzum," described as creatures with little round bodies and long, spindly legs, and I thought it was odd because there were Yuzzem (with an 'e') in "Splinter," but these were serious bad-ass guys – one of them turns an Imperial into that glistening double-handful of slop – that I always pictured as a cross between a Wookiee and an orangutan.

I was always confused, though, by a bit near the end of the book. Luke and Vader have just been Force-beating the snot out of each other: Vader's lost an arm and is staggering around, Luke's in an exhausted heap on the ground. Then comes this line: *"I'm sorry," he murmured, turning his head to where the Princess lay crumpled on the temple floor. "I'm sorry, Leia. I loved you."* Problem is, the previous paragraphs are so packed with action and description going back and forth between farm boy and Sith Lord that it's not immediately clear who "he" is. For years, I assigned the line to Vader. (This was way before anybody knew the whole brother-sister-dad thing was going on.) It was only when I re-read the book in my late twenties that I realized it could have been – and in fact, probably was meant to be – Luke's line. I could go look it up in that comic version, I suppose, but I like keeping the memory of the mystery.

Oh, and one last thing: On the cover, Luke's hair is too long, and you can't see his face, so he looks like a girl. This also confused me when I was little.

"Splinter" was a relatively easy read for me, even at age eight. There were words I didn't know – "hirsute," for instance, and "troglodytes" – but it was still *Star Wars*, so I just kept on plowing through the pages.

The *Star Wars* novelization struck me as much tougher, probably because the opening of chapter one – "It was a vast, shining globe and it cast a light of lambent topaz into space – but it was not a sun." – immediately put me off my guard. What the hell? Where's the gigantic Star Destroyer? Where's the laser barrage and the explosions? How am I supposed to know what's going on without those yellow-lettered paragraphs floating past? And what's "lambent topaz" mean anyway?

I was also blasted by the prologue, which ended with the designation, "From the First Saga, Journal of the Whills." Huh? What's this "first saga" thing? Decades later, when I was in college, I even searched for "Journal of the Whills" in the Bowling Green State University library's computer system, since this was before the Internet as we know it. Part of me is still a little tweaked that 30 years and a prequel trilogy and a cargo hold of *Star Wars* spinoffs later, there's no more mention of the Whills, but then again, since Episodes I-III gave us midichlorians, I suppose there's nothing wrong with an unanswered question or two.

Another thing that stuck with me from the *Star Wars* novelization is the Jabba the Hutt scene in Docking Bay 94, not because this bit wasn't in the movie, but because it was on the pages bracketing the book's glossy section of film photos. (I eventually tore those pages out – presumably so I could look at the pictures without the incredible hassle of actually opening the book.)

The third and slimmest volume in my paperback trilogy collected the first six issues of Marvel Comics' *Star Wars* printed in black and white. I saw this version before I saw the actual comics themselves and I was stunned when, at my friend Trevor's birthday party, I saw the explosion of colors – particularly in the two-thirds-page illustration of the Falcon's jump to hyperspace – in the giant-sized color edition he'd gotten.

The comic books did make it into our house eventually, because I think dad bought a bagged set of them, maybe in a couple three-packs. The taffy-pulled interpretation of Ben Kenobi's death by lightsaber kind of weirded me out, like the one I had in a Spider-Man Read-Along-Record book where the villain is transforming from a human to a lizard and there's a portrait where he's got a human face, but he's green and yellow.

Inspired by the Marvel *Star Wars*, one day I was coaching my friend Rick in our garage during what was supposed to be a re-creation of the Vader-Kenobi duel. We were wielding these miniature cues from a toy pool table, and I was trying to get him to play out the dialogue, only somehow he just wasn't getting the nuances right, so his delivery of Vader's "Your powers are weak, old man" was a lot closer to, say, Bruce Willis as John McClane in *Die Hard* – all hyperactivity and loud threat – than it was to James Earl Jones' slow and deadly onscreen taunts.

At school, I remember spending a rainy first-grade recess reading the *Star Wars* comics with a couple other kids. Along the back wall of our classroom was a set of orange and yellow cupboards, two rows high. The lower left corner space, though, was just an open cubbyhole area, and two of my friends and I sat in there reading *Star Wars*. (That cubby is also where I learned the trick of breaking crayons with my middle three fingers and a slap on the leg. Went through a box of 64 in one sitting.)

My daughter attended that same elementary school and had first grade in that same classroom. The cupboards are still there, including the one with different hinges on its door because I broke the original set by swinging on it. The cubby was still there, too: It had one of those small two-drawer filing cabinets in it, which filled the entire space. I couldn't have squeezed myself in there these days, much less two pals and a set of comic books.

I was never a comics kid except for *Star Wars*, and even that didn't last very long. I had the next six issues, I think, that continued the heroes' stories beyond the original movie, but really wasn't in for the long haul.

I do remember an issue starring Han and Chewbacca and a rabbit-alien and a guy named Don Wan Kihotay (imagine my astonishment in high school at realizing this had been a literary reference). And there were others with a red-bearded space pirate and a girl pirate named Jolli, who lives in my brain in a flashback sequence showing her as a little girl watching her father leave his family behind, and then in her death scene, when Han plants a kiss on her cold lips.

I took these comics on a family vacation to Myrtle Beach, I think, and read them in the back seat of the car during the drive down. I was reading that bit about Jolli when my aunt – the same one who'd given me the paperbacks – asked my if I ever read any "regular" comics. Like, you know, "Archie." I did have a couple of those little volumes of Archie and Jughead, but *Star Wars* had its hooks in me pretty damn deep by this point and was first choice from here on out.

Lighter *Star Wars* reading was also out there: The Activity Books (I had the Chewbacca edition, and either the Luke or Vader one, too) with their pencil-and-paper brainteasers and suggestions for games like "Rebellion," which requires a regular deck of Earth-made playing cards and bears a striking resemblance to "War."

My favorite kids' book, though, was "*Star Wars*: The Mystery of the Rebellious Robot." Lots of pictures, simple plot, spaceships and droids gone bonkers and pesky Jawas galore. But it was the pictures that sold this one: These weren't bland renditions or just airbrushed versions inspired by movie stills. These were squiggly and cartoony caricatures that are still just a ton of fun.

One of the neatest things I've been able to do as a writer was track down the illustrator of that book, Mark Corcoran, with the notion of writing a feature on the book's 25th anniversary back in 2004. I wrote him a letter, we had a few phone chats, and I turned it into an article for TheForce.net.

I even bought one of the original "Rebellious Robot" illustrations for the book from Mark. It's one of my favorite pieces of *Star Wars*, kept a shelf or two above the one where you'll find the paperback copy I had as a kid.

Paper's not as durable as action figure plastic, but I have almost all of my *Star Wars* books from those days, my name fat-penciled inside their front covers, worn soft and faded, spines glazed with yellow, brittle tape, pages hardly held in place. I could find better copies on eBay or through other collectors, or buy reprints from Amazon or Barnes & Noble, but somehow, that would change the stories I remember.

Proof of Purchase

At one point, I thought it would be cool to re-invent my *Star Wars* storybook by cutting out all the pictures and pasting them together on new pages, then doing the same thing with the text. That way all the great pictures of spaceships and aliens would be grouped together, undisturbed by those boring columns of type.

I honestly don't remember if I actually managed to start cutting up my book before realizing that *pages are printed on both sides*, and this plan wouldn't work.

Two movies later, when I should have known better, similarly poor planning led me to staple all my red-border *Return of the Jedi* cards to a piece of poster board, leaving gaps for the ones I didn't have. Never mind that I didn't know whether to leave vertically-oriented or horizontally-turned spaces: The thing already looked like crap. And no, I never filled it all in.

Collect All 21!

When I was little, getting *Star Wars* stuff was great. And yet it's easier to remember the deep-seated *wanting* of the toys – and I mean really, relive-the-feeling-physically remember, like the memories of wrecking my bicycle or slicing my knee open – than it is to recall the actual getting or having.

Having *Star Wars* stuff really only increased the wanting. Have you looked at a modern-era *Star Wars* figure? Hasbro pictures 10, maybe 12 other figures on the packaging. Know why? Because since relaunching the *Star Wars* toy line in the mid-1990s, there have literally been hundreds of *Star Wars* figures produced. Having them all, though possible, isn't even a practical marketing ploy anymore. But as a kid, imagining the day when you had every *Star Wars* guy (That was the generic term we used: "guys," as in, "Should I bring my *Star Wars* guys over?" Never "action figures.") was a pastime rooted in reality. Even up through *Return of the Jedi*, Kenner never lost sight of that, showing every figure on every cardback and encouraging us to "Collect all 92!"

In the fall of 1978, I started second grade and had an assigned seat on the bus with two other guys who were also *Star Wars* fans. (We were still small enough to sit three to a seat, which made for at least one less-than-fun ride home when one of my seatmates barfed up his school-cafeteria mac-and-cheese all over the seatback in front of us. The three of us rotated spots daily, and that incident really made sitting in the middle no fun because the resulting stain never fully faded and stared you right in the face.) We regularly used to flip through our Topps *Star Wars* trading cards or sneak a figure or two into our bookbags. And then one day, Doug (I think) brought the backing card to a new *Star Wars* guy he'd just gotten, and what I saw on the back of the package made me sugar-buzz hyper: Eight new *Star Wars* guys.

And what a bunch. As cool as the original dozen figures were, even with the "exciting" figures like Chewbacca and Darth Vader, it was a pretty bland color palette – the bright spot was the lemon-yellow hair on Luke's head, unless you counted the lightsabers. Lots of black and white and gray and shades of brown. Even shiny gold C-3PO was kind of subdued. These new guys, though, stood out on the back of the package as bright as Life Savers: Luke in his orange X-Wing flight suit; sun-struck-grass green Greedo; bright red accented R5-D4 and squat, dark red Snaggletooth. OhmanohmanohMAN I had to get those guys! Hammerhead! Power Droid! Death Star Droid and Walrus Man!

Half the new guys were from the famous scene in the cantina, which you could now re-create in your own home, thanks to the playset advertised on the package too.

To this day, the thrill of seeing those new guys resonates: Looking at one of the old cardbacks I have, that particular version with the 8 new figures ("Collect all 20!"), I can feel the distant thrum of gut butterflies, like the vertigo you get sitting high in an arena and looking out at the girders supporting the roof.

After school, I begged begged begged my Dad to take me to Kmart to get one of the new guys, any one, I didn't care which – I'd have even been happy with Power Droid, even though he was about the lamest of the bunch – because that's where the kid on the bus said they were. Whether it was that day or the next, it wasn't long before Dad and I made the five-minute drive to the North Canton Kmart and I made for the toy aisles, only to find nothing new at all among the *Star Wars* shelves. Zippo. Same old Stormtroopers and Jawas and Hans and Lukes. And those gut butterflies fell silently in a heap.

Whether because he felt bad for me or because I whined a lot, Dad bought me a couple *Battlestar Galactica* figures instead: A four-armed Ovion and the purple lizard-esque Imperious Leader. (I wanted funny-looking aliens, after all.) They were weird and felt chunky, like preschool toys, next to the neat, straight-limbed *Star Wars* guys at home. I kept them for years anyway.

That Kmart, though completely overhauled inside, is still there, and I can still picture where the *Star Wars* toys were, and remember fishing frantically through the shelves trying to find a new figure.

As with the first bunch of *Star Wars* guys, I remember the heartache of not getting them right away much more than I remember the times I actually got them. Eventually, though, I did, and of course, needing a properly wretched hive of scum and villainy for these guys to hang out in, I got the Cantina Playset. This is another toy I still have, although the backdrop is a full-color copy and the swing-open saloon-style doors are long gone, and I don't think any of the action levers work anymore. All that really survived was the molded plastic base with its semicircular bar and that round table that sat in the back booth.

Action levers were a great thing about the Kenner playsets: You'd stand one figure atop a small slot in the base, then put another figure on a little platform nearby. Pushing a lever rotated the platform and then, at a certain point, activated a little spring-loaded fin that would pop up through the slot and make the first figure tip over. Instant barfight! (Or Jawa attack or Stormtrooper ambush or whatever.)

I used to meticulously set up Han and Greedo in that back booth of the Cantina, positioning them so that Han would draw his bead on the bounty hunter just as the spring popped into position, sending the bad guy sprawling. I'd even try to get Greedo to fall across the table, since the Kenner designers had gone to the trouble of printing the image of a spilled drink on the tabletop's decal.

During this second surge of *Star Wars* stuff, my family and I paid a visit to grandma over in Upper Sandusky, Ohio. Among Upper Sandusky's claims to fame are an old Wyandot Indian mill, a cemetery headstone recognized by Ripley's Believe It or Not because it says "Feb. 31", and being the home of a character in the Infocom text adventure "Leather Goddesses of Phobos" when those games were the computer geek rage in the 1980s.

My grandma was a librarian at the Carnegie Public Library in Upper, so I spent a lot of time there. Classic old brick building with narrow staircases and a basement that felt dark all the time. I can almost imagine into existence the wood and plaster and book-page smell of the place.

Up near the front door was a glass case where people would display collections of things, and on one visit, my grandma wanted me to see the collection of *Star Wars* toys in there. And that's where I saw something that would confound me for years: an action figure that looked kind of like the short, red-suited Snaggletooth I had – same face, same hands, same belt buckle design – but this guy was tall and blue and had shiny silver moon boots.

Now, of course, this guy's well-known as the Blue Snaggletooth, product of a Sears exclusive Cantina set and a Kenner design fluke. I wouldn't learn that, though, until I was in my early twenties. Right then, I was just too fascinated and jealous and mesmerized. I stared at this thing, trying to figure out what it was and where it had come from and why wasn't it in any of the Kenner *Star Wars* catalog booklets and how, good God, could I get my hands on one? (Wouldn't happen, by the way, until I was married and living in Florida almost 20 years later, and that was an $80 purchase I scrimped for months to buy. Eighty bucks for a *Star Wars* guy! Somewhere, 7-year-old me was passed out in shock.) I remember telling my friends about it, and none of them had seen or heard of one of these things either, and I probably sounded like that kid on my street talking about his supposed Grand Moff Tarkin toothbrush. It didn't help that I never saw another Blue Snaggletooth as a kid.

This second wave of *Star Wars* toys also included the Droid Factory Playset, which was, I think, the first toy made for the action figure line that didn't have an on-screen counterpart. In fact, you didn't need any action figures at all to play with it – the point really seemed to be putting together robots, most of which really didn't look like they belonged in *Star Wars* at all. There was a book of blueprints to follow if you wanted, including instructions for a monster droid that used every single piece in the playset, and was impressive from that standpoint but was really a pretty goofy-looking thing when it was done. You could even build an R2-D2 that included his third leg, which put it a step ahead of the regular action figure, although it also fell apart pretty easily. The factory had axles and wheels and arms and skinny tubing and little rubber pegs that held stuff together, and I'm sure I started losing parts about five minutes after I opened it.

Now, with all these new guys, I had the full potential for a real battle royale. A laser-gun massacre in plastic. So I divvied them up one afternoon up in my room – good guys vs. bad guys, with the unknowns (most of the Cantina guys and extra droids) split up between both sides. For some reason, I set this up like you sometimes see pre-American Revolution battles illustrated: Two forces at a standstill, face-to-face. I lined up the good guys in a row on the orange-brown carpet of my room, and had the bad guys hunkered down in a plastic old-style lunch pail propped open and standing on its lower front edge, making a two-level "base." (I never had a real case for my *Star Wars* guys, so I'm pretty sure that lunch pail was also one of the many places I kept them when I wasn't playing with them.) All the figures were sitting, since it was too hard to make them stand on their own.

Then the firing began.

I handled all the dialogue and all the taunts and all the final, dying words and all the laser noises and all the explosions. One by one, my *Star Wars* guys perished. (I don't seem to recall any lightsaber fights, actually. Back then, we didn't know how kick-ass Jedis and Sith could be. They were just swordfighters, no matter how clumsy and random they thought blasters were.) I was a very nearly equal-opportunity battle god, inflicting heavy casualties on both sides.

When the smoke cleared, and the camera panned up from the carnage of the battlefield – yes, I actually used my hands to frame the shot as if I were watching it on a movie screen – there were just two survivors. The good guys had won, but only Luke and either Han or Chewbacca (time and trauma of the battle have scarred my memory) had lived to tell the tale.

There was, of course, one more figure in the original *Star Wars* line: Boba Fett. This new mystery guy who showed up for a few minutes in the "*Star Wars* Holiday Special," before the release of *The Empire Strikes Back*. Some kids ordered him as a bonus figure in the mail, but I got my Boba Fett the old-fashioned way: at Click's. I couldn't believe my luck when I found this incredibly cool enigma of a guy who, judging by the illustration on the package, could shoot fireballs from his wrist guns and maybe even fly using his rocket pack. It must have been autumn, because Dad said I could get it, but I'd have to make a choice: Either Boba would stay in storage until my birthday or Christmas, or I could open it up and play with it right away but pay Dad back for it.

I couldn't wait. When I got home, I scraped together the money from my room and ripped open that Boba Fett package and had that masked bad-ass flying all over the house, up and down the stairs, arms extended Superman-style and unleashing carnage from his flamethrowers. I even roped Dad in for a few minutes, who role-played Han and taunted this new arrival to the house by nicknaming him "Bubble Head." Boba fried him for that one. This was at least a half hour of pure Kenner-drenaline.

And then I crashed hard from the high and wanted my two bucks back, knowing that Fett would be mine again soon anyway. I put the figure back on the card, placed the bubble over him even though I'd completely torn it off the package and went to Dad, meek and regretful. But there was no going back on the deal. I was sad for a bit, but then probably realized that now I wouldn't be heading into my birthday already knowing what one of my presents was, and besides, did I mention that I had a brand new Boba Fett?

It's only been as I've been writing this essay that I've realized what a milestone and turning point that action figure marked.

When I walked out of Click's into that sunny afternoon, soon to be two bucks lighter, I had done it.

I had Collected All 21. The next figures would come out with the release of *Empire*, and 21 became 32 and then 41 and 45 and 48, and the figures went up from $1.75 to $2.50 and then $3.00 and four bucks and change and there were just too many to get.

But for a few months in there, I could look at the back of any Kenner *Star Wars* action figure package and put a magic-marker X over every one pictured.

It was the last time I could ever say that I had all the *Star Wars* guys.

Proof of Purchase

Jake came over to spend the night once – I figure this was around 1980 – and my parents were going next door to play Scrabble or cards or something with our neighbors. We went along because, looking back, I guess Mom and Dad just didn't trust a couple 9-year-old boys alone for a couple hours.

Jake had one of those Kenner "Give-A-Show" projectors: kind of an oversized flashlight with a slot where you slipped filmstrips through frame-by-frame, and he'd brought it along, along with the *Empire Strikes Back* filmstrips.

They were unintentionally hilarious. The drawings were very cartoony and oversimplified, which makes the fact that they included the torture rack scene even more hysterical. As I remember it, in the picture, Vader's standing next to Han and saying something like, "The Empire doesn't like troublemakers." This had us howling.

A Certain Point of View:
Imaginations in Hyperdrive

One of the best things about being the age I was when *Star Wars* came out was that the world still seemed like a pretty vast place. Details got foggy if you were talking about somewhere beyond the end of my street or a time further back than about a year and a half. Facts were facts until proven otherwise, and stories were taken at face value.

Star Wars gave birth to galaxies of conjecture.

Rumors flew, for instance, around the whole mystery of the "Episode IV" designation, which, along with stuff like the "Journal of the Whills" reference in the beginning of the *Star Wars* novel, gave rise to the idea that other *Star Wars* movies had been made. We'd just never heard of them because we were only little kids, after all. I remember word going around the fledgling geek community that some movie theater in Kansas City was showing all 12 *Star Wars* movies. (Kansas City? Twelve? Where did we get this stuff?)

No matter. We ate it up and added our own stories to the mix.

Take the time when I was in first or second grade and I met Darth Vader: He came to the Belden Village Mall and set up shop at the center, in front of the O'Neill's department store and next to the era's requisite mall fountain. Like Santa Claus or the Easter Bunny, minus the blankets of fake snow and grass, and with a couple Stormtroopers flanking him in place of elves.

For years, I kept the glossy 8-by-10 publicity photo they passed out, which he signed for me in black magic marker. Just to be clear:

This wasn't James Earl Jones or David Prowse. This was DARTH VADER. And that's how he signed the picture, there at the mall's center, a short walk from the Hobby Center store where I'd gotten my first *Star Wars* figure – Vader, of course.

When I got to school and started talking about my meet-and-greet with the Dark Lord, this kid William said he'd seen Darth Vader at a mall, too.

Here's the deal with William: The kid may have been the only one in our class geekier than me. High, nasal voice, knew how to read words even I couldn't get ("chameleon" comes to mind). Had, like me, all but memorized the Marvel *Star Wars* comic adaptation and thus was able to explain things like why Princess Leia didn't give Chewbacca a medal at the end of the movie. (Because "Few space princesses are that tall.") Not a bad kid. We used to joke about mixing martinis on the playground. I have no idea why.

So William had his own "met Vader at the mall" story, only his went way beyond my handshake and a Darth Hancock. The mall he'd seen Vader at, William explained, had set up an entire *Star Wars* funhouse. And not only had he met Vader, but he'd actually ridden with the big guy in a replica of his TIE fighter cockpit. And where the front window was, there was a viewscreen showing the trench battle scenes from the movie, and Vader had menacingly told William to push the firing button, which he did, and that had been the shot that killed Luke's old pal Biggs. (Knowing Biggs' whole backstory was a dead giveaway of geekdom in those days, because it wasn't included in the movie. Only someone who'd read the books and comics would know he was Luke's best friend.)

I was insanely jealous. Where was this mall? I had to go! Yes, I bought William's story hook, line and Jawa and probably faithfully spread it around to other *Star Wars* fans.

William's tale I now chalk up to good-natured enthusiasm. Kevin's, though ... Kevin was just kind of a jerk.

This was a few years later. He rode my school bus and lived about a mile away, which was bike-riding distance, but too far to walk. Obnoxious, mean kid. Example: Near the end of my street growing up was a place we called the creek. Really just the meet-up of three roadside drainage ditches forming a pool probably two feet deep after the heaviest of rains, and maybe ten feet across. Summers, it used to breed so many frogs you could catch a dozen tadpoles just by dipping a bucket in the water. Kevin and I went there one day and he stuck a tadpole on the street and stepped on it, slowly, with the toe of his cowboy boot, until it burst. That stuck with me for longer than I wished.

Still, he liked *Star Wars*, which was something to talk about. (He also liked the Miami Dolphins and wore a teal-and-orange coat in winter.)

Sometime after *The Empire Strikes Back* came out, Kevin and I were on the bus talking about *Star Wars* toys, and I wondered why there was no Cloud City playset, with something where you could put a Han figure in and turn a knob to get a Carbonite Frozen Solo out the other side. (I was thinking at the time of those old *Star Trek* toys and their rotating-door "transporter" features.) So Kevin starts talking about a Cloud City set that he saw that had a Carbonite Freezing Chamber and a Torture Chamber – man, Han just didn't have a good day on Bespin – that would leave three little pin-dents on the chest of your favorite action figure.

Kevin must have claimed this belonged to a friend or cousin, because honestly, if he'd said he had it at his house, I'd have gone over and demanded to see it, tadpole murderer or not. (Now that I think about it, I think he had also at some point claimed to have seen a Grand Moff Tarkin action figure. Jerk.)

It wasn't gullibility. It was a belief in mystery and possibility, and I'd be lying if I said I didn't miss that in these days of endless spoilers and movie countdown websites.

Still, the *Star Wars* universe has kept expanding, with cartoon spinoffs and novels and comics and such, and remember: Long ago, Lucas was often quoted as saying the movie saga was a nine-chapter triple-trilogy. In fact, one of my friends knows a guy who's working on the story developments for parts seven, eight and nine.

Also, I've got a used *Star Wars* fun house to sell you.

Proof of Purchase

Mom surprised me and Mike D. with some *Empire Strikes Back* Presto Magix one afternoon, and we both went bonkers, tearing into the packages with their paper backgrounds and sheets of transfer stickers waiting to be put in place.

Mom grinned and said, "Don't I even get a 'decent?'" This threw me for awhile because I thought she was implying we were ungrateful and just hadn't completed her thought, as in "Don't I even get a decent thank-you?"

Later I realized that she was talking in our language of the time, which, for Mike and me, included using the word "decent" as an adjective meaning "cool." Occasionally, we'd even shorten this to "Deese!"

Yes, it sounds unbelievably silly, sure, but then again, consider: wicked, gnarly, radical, sweet...

Bounty Hunting:
A Pack-A-Day *Star Wars* Habit

Girls go to Jupiter

To get more stupider,

Boys go to Mars

To get more Star Wars *cards.*

Yes, it's supposed to end with "candy bars," but that's the way my seatmates and I sang it on the school bus in second grade.

I never kept my *Star Wars* cards in albums. There were always either tossed into a shoebox or, more often, just kept rubber-banded together. And we measured collections not by number or completeness of card sets, but in stack thickness. Saying someone had "200 cards" or even "all the yellow ones" didn't impress as much as if you said you knew someone with "about this many" *Star Wars* cards, and you held your fingers about four vertical inches apart.

I had a small bookshelf at home that had two sliding glass doors set into grooves along the front edges. One of these panes became the place for me to put the stickers I got from packs of *Star Wars* cards: Grand Moff Tarkin, C-3PO, a Tusken Raider. When I bought other kinds of cards, their stickers went there too, which is how a *Close Encounters* alien made it into the mix. I remember the earlier *Star Wars* stickers, the ones that were cut-outs of character heads outlined in bright colors, looking bizarre next to some of the later stickers that were rectangular and bordered with edges printed to look like film sprocket holes.

It was always a cool thing when Topps put out a new set of *Star Wars* cards. The blues, yellows and reds came first, I think, but I remember being particularly stoked by the orange cards when I found them in Finney's, the closest drugstore to our house.

Finney's sold all kinds of other cards, too: *Close Encounters of the Third Kind, Mork and Mindy.* I can remember being in the store with Rick one day – his parents had driven: Finney's wasn't within biking distance – to buy *Star Wars* cards. We had money for two packs each. Rick somehow convinced me to split my purchase and buy one *Star Wars* pack and one pack of Kiss – yes, the rock band – cards. Kiss did not appeal to me at all, but it was the 1970s, so I caved in, even though I was embarrassed to be buying them.

Rick was also the source of a big chunk of my early *Star Wars* card collection. He'd either bought or traded for a three-inch thick stack of green-bordered cards, and I bought them off him for fifty cents. I seem to think I got a Cleveland Browns 7-Up bottle in the deal, too, although that may have cost me another fifty cents. (From a sheer "get-more-*Star-Wars*-stuff" point of view, the trading cards had serious affordability working in their favor. My allowance wouldn't support regular trips to the store to buy action figures or toys, but I could almost always scrounge up enough change to buy a pack of cards on a moment's notice.)

The one *Star Wars* card that it seems everyone knows about now is the infamous green-bordered C-3PO #207 where he appears to have an extra appendage. A specifically male appendage. And it's standing proud. I never saw this card as a kid, but I found one decades later at a flea market, in with a small bunch of *Star Wars* cards on a table full of random junk. It cost me a buck, and it remains my one true flea market jackpot. (When I was in college, I found a statue of a monkey sitting on a pile of books, one labeled "Darwin," and pondering a human skull. It was $40, so I walked on by. Not five minutes later, I found the same thing literally one aisle over for five bucks. That's my second favorite flea market find.)

Collecting *Star Wars* cards was how I first learned the actors' names, which were printed on some of the publicity-photo kind of cards: Han Solo (Harrison Ford); Princess Leia (Carrie Fisher); Darth Vader (David Prowse). This last one caused a minor stir when I was over at Mike D.'s house and his parents were talking about an interview they'd seen on TV where somebody named James Earl Jones was talking about being Darth Vader, and it confused the hell out of me, because I knew for certain that Darth Vader was David Prowse. Said so on my green-bordered *Star Wars* cards. And Mike's parents were baffled because they had clearly heard James Earl Jones speaking specifically about the role. I don't know if we ever figured out we were both right until much later.

Getting "checklist" cards was a mixed blessing: On the one hand, you felt kind of ripped off because it didn't have a cool picture on the front, or a puzzle piece or trivia on the back. On the other hand, now you had a way to see which cards you had and which you needed.

Once, I was showing my *Star Wars* cards to a girl at school I had a crush on. I'm thinking first or second grade. One card showed Han Solo leaning back in the cantina booth, and it was captioned, "Cornered by Greedo!" Maybe I'd only seen the movie once at that point, or maybe I was just overcome by this girl actually talking to me, and I couldn't concentrate properly with her head of long dark hair so close by. Either way, my explanation of the caption was that Darth Vader, being such a horrible villain, was obviously greedy, earning him the nickname "Greedo."

Never mind that Han and Vader were never even onscreen together in *Star Wars*, much less hashing things out in a dingy bar booth.

While I only remember ever buying *Star Wars* cards in individual packs, by the time *The Empire Strikes Back* cards came out, they were selling them in three-packs, only they came without the gum.

The first *Empire* cards were the red-bordered set, and I remember that these were different from the *Star Wars* cards in that on the back, instead of the printed puzzle pieces, they had paragraphs describing the scene on the front. And there were little "teasers" to the next card, so the series actually told the story pretty much as the movie did.

My friends and I were particularly fascinated by one card: #90, "The Ordeal," which showed Han on the torture rack in Cloud City. We were morbidly intrigued by that bit of the movie. Maybe it was the spookiness of that machine, with its flashing lights and electric shock noises, or maybe that it got Han Freaking Solo to just howl in pain from behind a closed door. It seems pretty tame by just about any standard today, but man, it stuck in my head when I was nine. I remember when another kid at school brought his "Ordeal" card and we clustered around him during recess to look at it. (In the second, blue-bordered set of *Empire* cards, a similar card of this scene was called "Han's Torment.")

My friend Jake and I also snickered a lot over card #67, the scene where C-3PO interrupts Han and Leia's first kiss, because the caption on the front read, "Pardon me sir, but … ohhh!" At that age, while make-out scenes in movies were disgusting if your parents were around, references to them were clearly playground-talk fodder. Our laughter was a more innocent version of the "bwomp-chicka-bwow-wooow" porn music jokes that came with high school and college.

I was 12 by the time *Return of the Jedi* came out, and while I was as big a *Star Wars* fan as ever, I was reaching a point where getting all the toys wasn't as big a deal. The trading cards, though, still appealed to me. I remember going up to the flea market with my mom and brothers in the summer once, and none of the trading card booths there had any of the still-new *Jedi* cards, so I decide to walk to the nearest drugstore to search.

I don't remember the name of the store, but it was about a half-mile away, in a shopping plaza where there was an IGA and a Fisher's Big Wheel department store. To get there, I hiked east on Route 619, a fairly busy street with no sidewalks, past the concrete-and-gravel business and the barn that housed the hobby and craft shop (which had sold Dungeons & Dragons stuff until the local churches threatened to boycott the place), and the gas station, and it was sunny and hot.

And the drugstore didn't even have any *Jedi* cards. I wound up buying one of those "Official Collector's Edition" *Jedi* magazine/program things, though, so it wasn't an entirely wasted trip.

Getting cards was always about the collecting – the hunting and comparing and swapping – rather than achieving a full set. It was about the tactile experience of tearing into the wax paper, chewing that brittle, crunchy gum into something half-palatable, and flipping through the cards to see what you got and piling the doubles off to the side. It was buying a couple packs at a time, but never going someplace like a comic shop and asking for a whole unopened box.

I don't know that I ever did assemble a whole series of any of the *Star Wars* cards as a kid, although enough of my *Empire* cards survived until I reached a point as an adult where I was back into collecting, and I was able to piece together the red and blue series with some buys over the Internet. And when I did get them, I stacked them all in a pile and was surprised to find how my hands still held the muscle memory of cupping the cards in my left hand and thumbing them over into my right as my eyes flicked over each image. All I was missing was the gum.

Proof of Purchase

In fourth grade, our English teacher had us compose letters to authors, and I remember my friend Mike S. writing to Brian Daley about the book "Han Solo's Revenge."

"How come," Mike wrote, "on the cover, it looks like Han's going to shoot Chewie?"

I don't think he ever got an answer.

Along A Different Path:
Taking *Star Wars* into Our Own Hands

I have a copy of Marvel Comics' *Star Wars* issue #5 framed on my wall. Classic example of artistic license on the cover: nothing like what you saw in the movie, but incredibly cool anyway. The Rebel Base hangar's taking direct fire from the Death Star, these fat green lasers shattering walls into rubble; Chewbacca and Luke are charging toward the Millennium Falcon; Han's waving his blaster over his head (Seriously: Why? It's the DEATH. STAR.) and shouting, "It's too late, kid! *We're finished!*"

Mounted next to this comic book is a yellowed drawing in pencil, crayon and magic marker. I can still remember working on this when I was six or seven, concentrating hard on the details and being disappointed that my art didn't exactly measure up next to the comic's. Blocky and balloon-headed, Luke, Han and Chewie are at the bottom like they're in a police lineup. None of them have elbows or knees, and their legs look like moon boots. Above them hovers a stark white crayon Death Star criss-crossed by red marker lines and a dead-center circle that represents its planet-killing weapon. At least I got the fat green lasers right.

I copied Luke's dialogue straight from the Marvel cover – "Hurry CHeWBacca! We're Being attaCKeD By the Death Star!" – but also gave Chewie a voice. He's saying "gRRRRRR!" and because his word balloon is tall and carrot-shaped it looks like the kind of thing you'd use to illustrate a growling bear charging off a cliff.

Han's dialogue, though, had me pumped, because within his word balloon is my own craft at work: "There's no Time KiD! we're Doomed for sure!" The last four words are lettered like ice cream squished into the bottom of a cone.

Compare and contrast, class:

"It's too late, kid! *We're finished!*"

"There's no Time KiD! we're Doomed for sure!"

Now *that's* a rewrite.

Another drawing from about the same time has C-3PO and R2-D2 in what's clearly supposed to be the Tatooine desert, but with a funky green and red Dr. Seussian plant thing growing on a cliff above them.

See, from the very beginning, I wanted to put my own fingerprints on *Star Wars*.

I associate a big part of this "make it our own" philosophy with my friend Jacob.

Jake moved to our school district in second grade, I think. We were good buddies in third grade and best friends by fourth, which was the last year we went to school together because his dad worked in the lumber business and they moved to Virginia.

So we met post-*Star Wars*, pre-*Empire*.

I always thought Jake was a lucky sonofabitch because he had two grandmas who seemed to be in a perpetual race to see who could buy him more *Star Wars* guys. He was the only kid I know who had some of the giant action figures, and when *Empire* figures started coming out Jake was the first kid I knew who had some. The guy had *two* Yodas (one from each grandma) before I'd ever even seen the little green Jedi master in a store.

Sometime in the 1980-81 school year, our English teacher, Mrs. Yoder, told us to partner up and write a story. I remember the exact phrasing of Jake's idea: "The continuation of *The Empire Strikes Back*." Too daunting for me, and we didn't wind up doing it, but that desire to have some storytelling fun in George Lucas' world was there.

It was just such a damn fun place to play.

Jake and I stayed in touch after he moved away the summer before fifth grade, and a couple years later, he came to Florida one spring break with me and my family.

One of the best things about our Florida vacations was that my parents used to drive non-stop overnight from Ohio. Because I'm seven years older than my middle brother, Nick, I was allowed to bring a friend, and I loved staying up late into the night talking and listening to music on our boom boxes, falling asleep for an hour or two here and there, feeling the air outside change in temperature and taste.

The year Jake came along, I'd brought a cassette tape of the read-along *Empire Strikes Back* storybook for some reason – I was too old for it, so maybe I had it for my little brothers – and on the drive home, Jake and I started messing around with it, putting pieces of paper over the recording-prevention notches on the cassette and adding our own yuks.

I think it started with a joke about Emperor Ovaltine. (This was after *Return of the Jedi*, so we knew the Emperor's name – Palpatine – by now.) That led us to the likes of Admiral Snackbar and Land O'Lakes Calrissian. And so we populated our parody, recorded piecemeal over the existing story of *Empire*.

We began with a few simple phrase changes.

"There is a great disturbance –" the creepy Emperor's hologram intoned, and then you'd hear this click and rattle while we paused the tape and hit "record," and then Jake's impression of the Emperor finished with "– in the plumbing system."

My turn. Vader: "He will join us –" *clickclickrattle* "– or be flushed, my master." (Yeah, we middle school boys always went for the highbrow humor.) Later on, Han's Cloud City carbon freeze became immersion in a vat of bubble gum.

Eventually, these gags just descended into total chaos as we recorded over bigger and bigger chunks of the original story recording. By the time R2-D2 was attacking C-3PO for abandoning the script to pitch his new breakfast cereal, we were in freaking *hysterics*, clutching our guts, stifling laughter during the tapings, bursting into howls with tears running down our faces as soon as we hit the "stop" button. Jake peed his pants a little bit he was cracking up so hard, and of course, I had to have my little brother announce it into the tape recorder, earning me a not-too-hard punch in the mouth and a bit of a bloody lip from Jake, even though we were both still laughing.

That tape got lost somewhere over the years, but I know it never got erased.

As much as we loved *Star Wars*, we still loved making fun of it.

Jake moved to Cincinnati after being in Virginia for a couple years, and I remember visiting him for a week one summer. Those shiny silver paint pens were popular at the time, and we did a vandalism number on his *Jedi* storybook, adding the usual moustaches and goatees and devils' horns and stuff like that.

When I was in middle school, I fished our family's old 8mm movie camera out of the crawlspace, shelled out my allowance for batteries and a light bulb and tried to make my own *Star Wars* films.

One winter, I took it outside in the snow, dug a makeshift Death Star trench – I added twists and turns to make it, you know, more exciting – and then filmed my own point-of-view attack run, never thinking that, *duh*, I was holding the camera by its handle – in other words, upside down.

I was a little more successful with the flick I made using my little brothers' Scout Walker. I managed to do some fairly steady stop-motion animation of the AT-ST's head rotating back and forth, its side guns twitching up and down, and then I had my brother Adam work its legs, stomping them up and down while I shot a close-up. Then we stop-motioned the top hatch opening and a Scout Trooper emerging (okay, he didn't so much "emerge" as he popped into existence from one frame to the next) and then – gasp! – quick cut to a skyward shot and a streaking meteor that was, in actuality, a lava rock my parents had brought me back from their 15th anniversary trip to Hawaii. And again, not so much streaking against the sky as being dropped by my brother with my textured white ceiling in the background.

Poor trooper never saw it coming. Caught it on the noggin, and… *as the black haze closed in on his battle-scarred mind, he barely felt his walker toppling, its legs crumpling, never to stride into war again.*

Aaaaaaaaand – scene.

The four-minute film reel containing this 30- or 40-second masterpiece survived long enough to make it onto a DVD we compiled as a Christmas present for Mom a couple decades later. Holding up the cardboard sign labeled "Assistant: Adam Booth," – I'd taken top billing as director and cameraman, naturally – my youngest brother looks like he's squinting into binary suns, the lamp on the movie camera's so freaking bright. We actually melted a tennis-ball-sized circle of carpet during filming when I accidentally put the bulb housing on the floor after a shot.

Another time, I set up an even more complex and special-effects-driven scene in the basement, though I didn't bother filming it.

Using some straws taped to the underside of the *Jedi*-era orange-brown AST-5 mini-rig and a couple pieces of string stretched from the ceiling near one end of the basement to a spot near the floor at the other end, I set up a glide path for our heroic pilot. (Playing "Heroic Pilot" in tonight's production is "X-Wing Luke," whose previous credits include Battle of the Lunchbox and Kitchen Death Run II.)

Our basement had one of those suspended ceilings made of foam tiles supported by a metal framework. (Once, when my little brothers were going through a phase collecting these StarCom toys that all had magnets in them, my buddy Aaron and I stuck every one of their action figures and spaceships to the metal ceiling bars. It looked like one of those old futuristic science paintings with astronauts walking upside down next to their rockets parked on spaceports in zero-G.) These ceiling supports came in handy during Heroic Pilot's descent, because they gave me places to anchor the lengths of sewing thread I tied, respectively, to the ship's detachable cockpit and to our hero himself.

At the lower end of the flight path, I set up a couple pillows to serve as a gun emplacement for my Death Star's turret cannon. (Missing its entire front end, this was the last remaining piece of that once-glorious playset. Space war is hell.)

So, I take the ship up to the highest point of its flight path, and the stage is set: *Our hero, under heavy Imperial fire from the hidden nest of laser cannons, finds his ship has taken one shot too many and is going down.* (Release the AST-5, and it starts its dive, hidden straws slipping smoothly over the string.)

Feverishly wrestling with the controls, Heroic Pilot makes a final adjustment before punching the eject button, sending the overhead glass whipping into the atmosphere, lost in the roar of his wake. (The thread tied to the cockpit tightens and yanks the plastic piece free of the ship, which continues its descent.)

Flicking his eyes downward, he squints into the hail of lasers from the rapidly-nearing turret before muttering a quick curse. He pulls one more lever and rockets from his ship as the boosters fire beneath him. (Thread tied to Heroic Pilot tightens, pulling him free of the doomed fighter.)

Inside the turret, two Imperial gunners realize, too late, that they've missed both their target and their chance for survival as the AST-5 plunges toward them. (Ship continues on its final run, crashing into the cannon and knocking it from the pillows.)

Our hero smiles grimly at the expanding fireball below, mutters a last goodbye to his ship, and scans the terrain for a place to land.

Aaaaaaaaand – scene.

Remember when I mentioned Jake's idea from fourth grade about writing a follow-up to *Empire?* Well, in late middle school or early high school, my buddy Aaron and I actually did dive pretty far into a post-*Return of the Jedi* project we called *Episode VII: The Emperor.* Aaron had a basic story idea to start things rolling, and I added my own ideas, and pretty soon, I was actually working on a screenplay and he had done some storyboards for it. We even had the opening crawl written. What we planned to do with all this, we had no idea, but it was an absolute blast. This is what I was working on when I'd shut myself in the walk-in closet with my boom box and mom's typewriter, *Star Wars* stuff on the walls and shelves around me.

We'd created a very cool scene, at least in our minds, opening our sequel with that climactic moment from *Jedi*, but showing the Emperor's fall from his point of view. Then we cut to the camera falling alongside him. (Yes, I swear, we thought all this out.) As he plunges, he tosses some of that Force Lightning from his hands and uses it to stop his fall by pushing it out against the walls. Sweat dripping into his eyes, he looks up toward the distant edge of the chasm … and the mothereffer *smiles.* Smiles and then, with a huge effort, brings his hands together in an explosion of Force Energy and disappears.

We kept all our notes and sketches and typed pages in a huge three-ring binder. It's long gone, and I'd trade my Blue Snaggletooth in a heartbeat if I could flip through those pages again.

Here's what I remember:

After that opening scene, we're off to the wedding preparations of Han and Leia, where everything's peachy except Luke's pretty messed up in the head and he bolts the festivities early to head to Dagobah to meditate on the Force.

We next see Palpatine in an underground throne room on a small, barren moon (Vadox? Vladox maybe?) that he's making over into yet another Death Star, since the first two worked out so well. Close up on his eyes, and then we see him snap his fingers. Across the galaxy, former stormtroopers drinking sullenly in cantinas or working in gritty underworld settings suddenly stop and cock their heads, as if they've heard ... *a call.*

So, Emperor's summoned an army and he raids the Good Guys' base during the Han/Leia wedding, and he kidnaps Leia and totally fries Han with a hefty dose of lightning. I vividly remember two of Aaron's sketched storyboards from this battle: One of the Emperor looking over his shoulder as a blaster bolt from Han bounces off his cloak, and one of Chewie standing, arms to the sky and howling, Han lying motionless at his feet. Beneath this, Aaron had written, "One shot, the end of a hero. Sorry, John."

Meanwhile, back at the ranch – that is, Dagobah – Luke's wandered into a funny place: a clearing of black sand with no living things inside its border. At the center is a black crystal globe on a pedestal. The glass is partially encased by fingers of stone. (True story: Years and years later, Aaron became a toy designer and worked on some comic book properties and related films. And in one of those movies, there's a snow globe prop that has this same kind of general look to it, because my old buddy Aaron designed it.) So this black ball thing, we decided, is the physical manifestation of the galaxy's Dark Side energy. And it's on Dagobah because as we all know (especially by now, but we had some idea even then, apparently), the Force loves its balance. So, ultimate good guy Yoda lives on the same planet as this pulsating Heart of Darkness.

Well, Luke gets word that things have gone to shit back home, so he rockets back for Han's funeral, and guess what he's learned in his meditations? Han, my friends, is only, as Miracle Max might say, Mostly Dead. Luke's able to bring him back with some digging-deep Light Side action, but it comes at a price, right? Because as he's tapping all this good karma, that ball back on Dagobah is buzzing. And when Han comes back to life, that thing friggin' explodes. It's all about the balance – you want the good stuff, you've got to deal with the bad stuff, and what was born out of that crystal was the darkest of dark knights: an empty Vader suit, walking around on its own, fueled by nothing but pure Dark Side badassedness.

It sounds cheesy as hell, I guess, but there's a lot in *Star Wars* that's cheesier. (Maybe I was tapping into this bizarre memory: When I was littler, someone had gotten me a big Darth Vader model kit with the glow-in-the-dark lightsaber and eyes, and his head had broken off and, I kid you not, rolled into the hole in our basement where the sump pump drained. That thing floated in there for awhile, and every so often I'd move the hole's cover aside and see Vader's pale greenish-white eyes and get the willies.)

Beyond all that, I can't remember much. I know Han and Luke wind up leading a raid on Vadox/Vladox and rescuing Leia, and that our ultimately super-cool ending was to have The Emperor get killed by none other than that phantom Vader. All about the balance, after all.

And yet, after some thought, Aaron and I ran into this problem: Vader sacrificed himself to save Luke and turn away from the Dark Side. If the Emperor's not dead, it means that sacrifice was for nothing. It bugged us. (And it still bugged me in the early 1990s when a reborn Emperor was the villain in the Dark Empire comics, even though that series helped re-ignite interest in the *Star Wars* universe.)

Still, in a weird way, it was fun for Aaron and I to see, even years later, that we hadn't been alone in some of our notions, and that we weren't the only ones who'd been thinking about putting our fingerprints on the saga.

Proof of Purchase

Long before Lego started selling *Star Wars* kits, I built my own Star Destroyer out of the things. Green and red and white and blue and with a single clear brick to serve as the bridge, it bristled with blocky laser cannons and had nothing on it that looked remotely pointy or menacing. But it was my Star Destroyer, dammit.

There is Another:
The *Empire* Era

The Empire Strikes Back is a special movie.

From a strictly cinematic standpoint, it's the best *Star Wars* flick in the bunch: It's a visual stunner, the script's genius, and the plot and its cliffhangers rock.

Of course, it runs deeper than that, because looking back, the *Empire* era was kind of my Golden Age of *Star Wars*.

For starters, *Empire* marked the first time I'd ever really paid attention to the idea of a sequel. That's right – I'm eight or nine years old, I'm obsessed with *Star Wars*, cut-out action-figure proofs-of-purchase are the coin of my realm, and what's that you say? They're making *another* one?!?! Oh, dear God.

Despite my rabid fandom, I didn't see *Empire* on opening day. Maybe not even opening weekend. For the life of me, I can't imagine why not, given that I'd been waiting for this movie for, at that point, a little less than a third of my *whole freaking life!*

Pre-internet, back when we lived in caves and watched our sitcoms on papyrus flip-animation books, there wasn't much in the way of movie speculation available to your average elementary-school kid. The closest thing I can think of was an issue of *National Geographic*'s *World* magazine which had a whole story on some of the special effects in the yet-to-be-released *Empire*. It came with this great poster of the Millennium Falcon being chased by a Star Destroyer – the familiar publicity shot with the green laser bolts ricocheting near her hull – and just a few photos in the article, but enough to get us really excited about what we were in for. Asteroids! Big metal animal-looking things! Luke and Vader going at it with lightsabers! (I kid you not – in one photo, there's a background light or something that looks, if you've got a little imagination and some hyperactivity, like a ghostly figure. My friends and I wondered if old dead Obi-Wan was making a spiritual comeback of sorts. He did, of course, but not in the way we'd been thinking.)

There was also a picture of the Falcon sitting on that Cloud City landing platform just after her arrival. I think it may have actually been in the background of a photo showing one of the matte-painting artists at work or something, because the picture was small enough that I couldn't actually tell it was the Falcon. Only later did I realize that what I'd thought was some kind of alien was actually Han and Chewie's starship. Even when I'm watching *Empire* for the umpteenth time, it's still easy to dredge up just enough of that 8-year-old me to see that landing platform as a creature with a Millennium Falcon-shaped head.

I remember seeing the previews, the lasting image being that shot of the Falcon careening sideways through a canyon, explosions in her wake. I was even enthralled by the new movie logo, with *The Empire Strikes Back* framed by a wraparound version of the old *Star Wars.* Incredibly cool. Even now, my favorite old-school toys and things are the pieces with that logo, because it still stirs those long-ago nerves of excitement and anticipation.

And then of course, there was the mystery of Boba Fett, tantalizingly offered in glorious full-color Kenner plastic well before we'd have any idea of just how ridiculously small a part he'd play onscreen.

Empire was also the first time we got to see a full-on *Star Wars* marketing and merchandising blitz leading up to a movie release, and we loved it. I don't think I ever did manage to collect all the stickers that went with that Burger King folder, or get all the fast-food chain's *ESB* glasses.

When the movie itself finally came out, I had to put up with hearing stuff from people who'd seen it – and man, oh man, the things I was hearing…

For starters, there was the glimpse of Vader's head. "All you can see is veins and stuff," was what I remember someone telling me, and I imagined it looking like a flesh-colored brain spidered with pulsing purplish-blue tendrils.

One of the older kids across the street was the first one to hit me with the "Darth Vader is Luke's dad" news. This rocked me, of course, but I wasn't mad about hearing it ahead of time. I was eight years old – all it did was make me want to see the movie more. I remember telling my Dad about it and him kind of shaking his head and saying something like, "Well, you never know. Maybe Darth Vader's just trying to trick Luke, so he won't kill him or something." Thinking back to the expression on Dad's face, I wonder if he wasn't maybe a little sad that the surprise had been spoiled.

A kid on my baseball team saw the movie before me, too. (Yes, I played baseball. No, not well. I was one of those outfielders who could probably count on one hand the number of times I actually touched the ball during a game because hardly anybody could hit that far.)

We were sitting in the cinder block dugout along the first base line at one of our late-afternoon games, and this kid was talking about *Empire*, which I seem to think I was going to go see that weekend. He had a nasal, smart-ass voice and was chewing gum open-mouthed, and I remember his nod when someone asked him, "Do they really show Han ripping the organs out of that monster?" The image that formed in my head was one of Solo in Cloud City, standing in front of a vague, hulking mass, tearing through its innards bare-handed and tossing pieces back over his shoulder like he was looking for a lost set of car keys in a pile of dirty laundry.

I'll never forget the day I finally got around to seeing the movie for myself.

The night before, my pal Jacob had come over to my house and my mom was going to drive us to Mellett Mall the next day and drop us off for a noon-ish showing. As it happened, some friends of our family were in town, and their son, a kid named Craig who was the same age as me and Jake, wound up coming over to spend the night, too.

So the three of us stayed up late goofing around and getting psyched about the movie and everything, but when time came to fall asleep, Craig said he wanted to go home. ("Home" being his grandparents house, where he and his family were staying.) Said he couldn't sleep and wouldn't even try. Didn't care that going home meant missing out, for the love o'Pete, on seeing *The Empire Strikes Back* the next day. He actually guilt-tripped me into going down into my parents' room at one-thirty in the morning and waking my mom up to ask her to take him back to his grandma's. Naturally – and I'm paraphrasing here – she said, "No way. Go to bed. Good night."

Next morning (yes, we'd finally fallen asleep, even Craig), we had breakfast, gathered up my friends' stuff and waited for mom to take us to the mall. Mom double-checked the show times in the newspaper and we headed out for a 12:15 matinee.

Got to the mall a few minutes before showtime. Went up to the ticket window to find that the movie had started at 12 o'clock. Son.Of.A.*Bitch.* Yep, that's right – the big reason I'll never forget the first time I saw *Empire* is because I missed the beginning. It was so disorienting, walking into that theater late, trying to find a seat and at the same time not wanting to take my eyes off the screen for more than a millisecond.

Thanks to previews, I figure we missed less than ten minutes. It's easier to recall what I *didn't* see the first time than to remember where exactly we came in: Missed the opening theme music and the yellow-lettered crawl; missed the Star Destroyer and the probe droid deployment; missed the Probot's impact on Hoth. I think we were there to see Luke get whacked by the Wampa. I *know* we were there for the belly-slitting scene, though, because I thought, "Well, that's hardly 'ripping the organs out.'"

A few other things stick with me from that first time, like confusing the curved-wing TIE Bomber with Vader's fighter and thought he was pursuing the Falcon through the asteroids himself. And when Luke was on Dagobah, Jake and I had to explain to Craig the meaning of Yoda's line "That is why you fail." (For my part, I utterly failed to realize that Luke was seeing his own face inside the Vader helmet.)

Later, in Cloud City, when they knocked over the block of carbonite containing Han, I remember thinking that he was "popping out" due to the impact of the block landing so hard.

And there was this awesome moment: During a pause in the lightsaber duel, while Luke was stalking Vader, I leaned over to Craig and whispered, "I hear somebody breeeaaa-thing –" and *right then* is when Vader jumped out of hiding with a huge downward slash of his saber.

When we walked out of the theater after the movie, I hardly remembered that we'd missed those first few minutes. It was still a couple weeks, at least, before I finally saw the movie in its entirety, and I was actually a little disappointed that the super-cool *Empire* movie logo wasn't in the opening titles. In the meantime, Jake had gone to see it with his parents and I dragged every possible detail about the movie's opening moments out of him. Not that there's a lot there to tell. Still, it was a few moments of *Star Wars* movie-time that I hadn't seen.

I did come away from that first viewing, though, with the two-dollar "Marvel Super Special Magazine" comics adaptation of the movie, since there was a special counter full of *Empire* merchandise set up there in the theater lobby. I read it until its cover came off and then some. I tracked down a copy within the last few years and was surprised at how the full-color pictures took me back and reminded me of all the differences between the comic and the movie. Luke's post-Wampa plaster face mask; the ice creatures attacking inside the Hoth base; the Jedi training on Dagobah where Luke tries to slice up a metal bar; the silhouette of Vader's bare head that actually makes it seem like he's got curly hair. (I'd also forgotten about the full-page black-and-white ad in the middle of the book: a scantily-clad space-warrior-princess flanked by a couple snarling Yeti-gorilla things advertising a new Marvel Masterpiece – Bizarre Adventures 2! Seeing it sparked the memory of wondering what this had to do with *Star Wars*.)

I still have the Kenner cardback from my first *Empire* action figure, which I was absolutely spastic to find for $2.38 on the pegs at Click's. I remember standing in front of this huge array of figures and digging through them, looking for some – *any* – of the new guys. Han Hoth, maybe, with that ultimately cool holster where you could actually hook his blaster; or the Bespin Luke with a lightsaber *and* a gun, and no more of this sword-embedded-in-the-arm goofiness. Or maybe even that almost-scary new Stormtrooper that looked like a ghost.

Gotta be honest: I can't remember if I saw these figures before I saw the movie or not. Looking at this cardback, it was early enough in Kenner's run that Yoda's not pictured on it, and I remember as a kid just dying to see what his action figure was going to look like.

So, you know what figure I wound up with? You know what the *only* new *Empire* figure Click's had was? FX-7, the cylinder-shaped medical droid. Oh, I was excited as hell just to have one of the new guys, but man, what a sucky figure. No feet. Zero play value. Screen time that makes IG-88's role look like Hamlet.

I tried to make him cooler than he was: pretending he could fly, opening and closing all those little plastic arms, extending his head and then turning it slightly so *it would stay up!!! Oooooooooooh!!!*

No good. He was still lame. Freaking Power Droid kicks this guy's ass.

But he was mine. Brand-new, *Empire Strikes Back* ecstasy mine.

In late third grade or early fourth, our class made "book plates." Little cards that said, "This book belongs to _____." I designed mine specifically for my Scholastic copy of *The Empire Strikes Back Storybook*. Two felt-pen TIE Fighters and an orange fireball. It's still tucked in there, even though there are only a couple brownish stripes where the scotch tape used to hold it in place. Speaking of the storybook, how big a rip-off was it to get this thing and find out it didn't have a single picture of a Snow Walker in it, unless you counted the close-up shot of Luke hanging underneath it? No bald Vader head, either. It was neat, though, that the picture of Luke and Leia staring out the window at the end shows a big pink and white nebula instead of the galaxy they showed in the movie. I remember that painting from the *World* magazine article, too.

I got not one but two Kenner mail-away toys during the *Empire* era: The Bossk figure, with his lumpy head and red eyes and a rifle that rested along his scaly forearm, and the Survival Kit that came with oxygen masks for spacers exploring giant slug innards, some Hoth-style backpacks and a knapsack for Luke to carry Yoda. Seeing those little white packages show up in the mailbox was pure joy.

For my birthday that year, my parents threw me a surprise party – Mom sent me to the basement before dinner to get a loaf of bread from the freezer and a bunch of my friends were down there waiting. We watched some Super 8mm movies from the library on the screen my Dad had set up, stuff like clips from the moon landing and maybe, I think, one of those seven-minute excerpts from *Star Wars*. Among the stuff I got was a Twin Pod Cloud Car, and my friends and I took turns flying it in front of the screen and noting that if you held it sideways, it looked kind of like one of those weird double-barrelled blasters from *The Black Hole*.

One of my friends' parents had wanted to get me a Tauntaun, but they couldn't find one in time for my birthday. A couple days later, before school one morning, I saw the Tauntaun box poking out from beneath a jacket on our kitchen table, and it took all my willpower to pretend I hadn't noticed it.

Besides the *Empire* figures, there were new ships: Boba Fett's Slave I (never had it); the Snowspeeder (had it – awesome pulsating laser guns *and* working harpoon/tow cable combo); Rebel Transport (never had it); Scout Walker – never had one (my brothers got the *Return of the Jedi* version a couple years later) but who gave a flying freighter about it because it was actually a laugher onscreen, dwarfed by its big brother terror machine, the Snow Walker. This beautiful four-legged monster (yeah, it's called an AT-AT, but "Walker" just sounded meaner) was *Empire*'s version of the Death Star, and I wanted one so freaking bad. Never got it.

On the other hand, I was lucky enough to get the two Hoth playsets Kenner put out: The Turret/Probot set ruled because it was the only way to get your hands on an Imperial Probe Droid, and the Imperial Attack Base was packed with levers and gadgets and clickers that did everything from turning a command center to rubble to collapsing a snow bridge. (The Rebel turret that came with the Probot set also had a detachable top that you could sit a guy in, and sometimes we used it as a mini-ship all by itself. Hell, if Kenner could make up an Imperial Attack Base that never existed in the movie, I was free to send my guys hovering around on miniature gunboats.)

I remember taking my Probe Droid apart and sneaking it to school in my jacket pocket one winter day, and me and Mike D. and Jake spent a whole recess making a little snowball "pod" to recreate the droid's plunge to the Hoth surface, and then playing with the robot in the piles of snow behind the chain-link kickball backstop.

Even the Twin Pod Cloud Car, which had about as much actual screen-time-related play value as FX-7, was great because it looked like nothing else in the *Star Wars* galaxy.

While the original Death Star playset was never to be surpassed, overall Kenner outdid itself with the *Empire* toy line. It was that sugar-rush giddiness of the first "new set" of *Star Wars* action figures all over again, times a hundred.

A couple years later, fifth grade was the last year before middle school, so it was the last year we did stuff like have Halloween parties and Christmas gift exchanges in our classrooms. The Christmas spending limit was about three dollars, but since my best friend Mike S. had drawn my name, I was surprised with an Imperial Commander figure, which had cost at least *four* dollars.

One of my favorite *Empire*-age presents, though, wasn't from the toy line at all.

I spent a lot of time in the fall of 1980 in the Belden Village Mall Waldenbooks coveting the shrink-wrapped stack of Ralph McQuarrie's *The Empire Strikes Back* portfolios. Made no secret of the fact I wanted this thing for Christmas. Bad.

And I remember without a doubt that my mom had pretty much assured me that she and Dad wouldn't be shelling out the bucks for it. I seem to remember price being a sticking point, like no way was Mom coughing up close to ten bucks for something I couldn't even *play* with.

As it happened, my mom's brother, Uncle Rob, spent that Christmas at our house. A little background: Uncle Rob was the youngest "grown-up" that I knew, which made him, you know, *cool*.

Uncle Rob, for example, had bought me a boxed set of "The Hobbit" and "The Lord of the Rings" books when I was in first grade. (I got through "The Hobbit" pretty easily, but I'll admit it was probably fourth or fifth or maybe even sixth grade before I got through the Ring saga itself. As a little kid, those chapters about "Many Meetings" and "The Council of Elrond" seem like they go *on* and *onnnn*.) I remember Uncle Rob being stoked about the then-new *Lord of the Rings* cartoon movie, and taking me to see it at the theater down by the Gold Circle store. He was going to buy me one of the Gollum posters they had for sale in the lobby, but we wound up seeing the last show of the day, and when we came out of the theater, the concession stand was closed.

When he'd visit our house, Uncle Rob would camp out on the floor of my room and we'd stay up late while he told me stories about growing up with my mom on the farm over in Upper Sandusky.

When I was a little older, he introduced me to the works of Isaac Asimov and theories about multiple universes and bending space and time.

And I remember going to Uncle Rob's college graduation and seeing the house where he lived at the time. They had a fish tank with a piranha in it and some record album cover set up behind it as a backdrop. (They also had the black-and-white cat that we'd given Uncle Rob as a kitten. He had wanted to call it "Felix," but his roommates had overruled him and gone with "Moon Puppy." This was the '70s, after all.)

So when Uncle Rob came to stay with us that Christmas, I knew things were going to be fun.

Christmas morning, I open up my present from Uncle Rob, and it's that *Empire Strikes Back* portfolio! I was just crazy excited because I had completely put it out of my mind, since, after all, Mom had shot it down. There weren't as many weird pre-production ideas in the *Empire* paintings as there had been in the *Star Wars* edition, but these prints were bigger, and the 25-picture collection came with an extra sheet of paper that had information about each one. Later, I sat on my bedroom floor looking through the whole stack again and again.

Almost thirty years later, I was watching a DVD made from our old home movies, and I rediscovered that actual moment: Me clutching my pack of *Empire* paintings in our green-carpeted living room, jumping up to hug Uncle Rob, who, naturally, earned himself a permanent spot on my Cool List.

Since it was the peak of *Empire*'s reign, and my little brothers would be the beneficiaries of the Ewok-laden *Jedi* holiday season, that was the last real *Star Wars* Christmas I had.

Proof of Purchase

In one of my middle school classes, we were having a discussion that involved everyone naming a famous person they admired. I picked Harrison Ford – duh, Indiana Jones AND Han Solo? This got me a dramatic sigh and an eye-roll from this girl Beth, who knew I was a *Star Wars* fan.

Who'd she pick?

Carrie Fisher.

Size Matters Not:
Star Wars on the Small Screen

For all the things that make *Star Wars* a truly big-screen experience, for first-generation fans, there was something special about seeing its spectacle on the television in the living room. There were no videotapes or DVDs or incessant cable channel showings. For years, we settled for bits and pieces of the movie caught in commercials or "Making of..." shows.

You saw *Star Wars* in a movie theater or you didn't see it at all.

The first *Star Wars*-related program I remember seeing on television was a science fiction special that was airing, I think, on PBS. The narrator was talking about visual effects in movies, and said something about how *2001: A Space Odyssey* had set a new standard that put things like the old Flash Gordon-type shows to shame. "Then," I remember him saying, "in 1977, George Lucas' *Star Wars...*" and something about a wholly new special effects experience, and suddenly the Death Star dogfight was on the television screen right in front of my face.

I was sitting on a footstool in my living room and feeling that roller-coaster swooping in my belly during the point-of-view shots of fighters diving into the trench and I swear I could hear the lasers sizzling past my ears and my heart was racing. (I tried to recapture that feeling once by running around the house like an X-Wing, with my hands positioned like horse blinders on either side of my eyes, then "diving" towards a photo of the Death Star trench in my *Star Wars* storybook. Not quite the same effect.)

I absolutely loved when stuff like that was on TV, especially the *Star Wars*-specific shows like "SPFX: The Empire Strikes Back," and "From *Star Wars* to *Jedi*: The Making of a Saga." I've seen the latter a lot over the years – I wore out two VHS copies of it – but I haven't seen "SPFX" since it aired back in 1980 or '81.

Star Wars even playing a passing role on another show was worth getting geeked up about, as in the case of Mark Hamill guest starring on "The Muppet Show," or seeing a *Star Wars* parody showcase showdown on "The Price is Right."

"The *Star Wars* Holiday Special" aired on my eighth birthday. (Not that I remember that specifically – it's just something I've learned in the years since.) I have only a fleeting recollection of the show taking place on the Wookiee home planet and there being an oddly uncool cantina scene. I've never watched it again, although I have seen the cartoon clip that introduced Boba Fett, which *is* kind of neat, and the bizarre Jefferson Starship music video that was part of the show, which is just terrible.

I can specifically remember the first time I saw *Star Wars*, the actual movie itself, on television, because it was the first time anyone saw *Star Wars* on broadcast television. It was early 1984, so I was 13 years old. I was on vacation in Vermont with my friend Trevor and his mom and stepdad, and we were staying in a condo at Killington.

And *Star Wars* being on TV was a big freaking deal. The commercial breaks were bracketed by short clips of interviews with the movie's cast and crew. As excited as I was about it in the weeks leading up to it, being on a ski trip, I'd forgotten all about it and we missed the beginning. Still, Trevor was a fan, too, so we camped ourselves on the fold-out couch beneath the shelf-mounted television set and had Coke and snacks and watched the best movie ever for the billionth time.

Star Wars on television figured into another ski trip years later when I was in high school. Aaron and I were at Seven Springs in Pennsylvania on a youth ski trip and the movie was on during our first night there. (Dinner had been so bad that we and our two roommates had a pizza delivered to our motel room and thought we were clever. The pizza guy showed up in a pie-laden truck and an order for just about every room in the place.) So we watched *Star Wars* and ate pizza, and Aaron and I got into an argument during the closing credits because I thought they'd rewritten the closing music slightly in order to cut away to a commercial. Aaron insisted they'd broken off at just the right beat within the existing score.

Watching it later – weeks or months, maybe – I realized he was right.

When *Return of the Jedi* came out, I set our family's boom box in front of the television so I could tape record of one of the movie trailers. (I did the same thing to make my first mix tapes, recording videos off MTV. To this day, if I hear Rush's "Distant Early Warning," right after Geddy Lee's cry of "Absalom! Absalom!," my mind inserts the sound of me saying "hi" to my mom as she came into the room.)

Two things happened sometime in my teenage years that forever changed the way I watched *Star Wars*: First, my family got cable. Then we got a VCR.

My first "watch-whenever-I-want" *Star Wars* collection was a single VHS tape with the movies recorded in the wrong order: *Star Wars*, then *Jedi*, then *Empire*. This got me by until I was in college and shelled out fifty dollars – holy crap, FIFTY DOLLARS – for the set's original boxed videocassette release.

I rarely sit down solely to watch the *Star Wars* movies anymore, though I go through the saga a couple times a year, popping the DVDs in while I'm doing stuff around the house or when I just want to chill and maybe doze a bit. The funny thing is, if I'm flipping through channels and I see one of the movies is airing, something stirs in me and I get a tiny leftover adrenaline rush from the years when catching *Star Wars* on television was a treasured rarity. I usually wind up watching at least a few minutes.

When Lucas was prepping to put the first trilogy back on the big screen under the Special Edition banners, the first trailer opened with a shot of a television and a single-speaker voice-over saying, "For an entire generation, people have experienced *Star Wars* the only way it's been possible: on the TV screen."

It hasn't always been a bad thing.

Proof of Purchase

Remember the final duel in *Return of the Jedi*, when Luke lets his anger get the best of him, and he just wails on Vader and then cuts his hand off, and then looks at his own black-gloved hand with the realization of what he could become? I'd forgotten that he'd put that glove on after getting shot in the hand on Tatooine, and the first time I saw the movie, I thought somehow that Vader's limb had actually grown onto Luke's arm, an actual physical transformation instead of the metaphor that was suggested.

What You Take With You:
Best Opening Night Ever

My movie-going experiences peaked when I was twelve years old.

Notice I'm not saying that when my mom and dad and brothers and my friend Mike S. and I went to *Return of the Jedi* on opening night that I saw the best movie ever. (Although if you'd asked me right after, I'd have probably said it was.)

I'm just saying that as an overall movie-going *experience,* seeing *Jedi* on May 25, 1983 makes an awfully damn convincing case for my top spot. (This is scored using a complicated formula of three years of anticipation plus best friend coming along plus pre-movie meal and line-waiting in the mall plus insanely-excited crowd multiplied by being a pre-teen *Star Wars* nutcase.)

First of all, you've got to remember the build-up: Three interminably long years before, we'd all staggered out of theaters having been slapped with the most insane cliffhanger ever – Han Solo frozen in carbonite and Luke wondering if Darth Vader's his dad.

In the meantime, I'd filled the gaps as best I could: Between 1980 and 1983 is when I read the first two of Brian Daley's Star Wars novels, "Han Solo's Revenge" and "Han Solo at Stars' End." I read them in the wrong order, and for some reason, I don't think I read "Han Solo and the Lost Legacy" until several years later.

There was also "The Jedi Master's Quizbook," which came out in 1982. I learned about it when they profiled the 11-year-old author on the TV show "That's Incredible." A couple days after it aired, Dad took me to the Waldenbooks at Belden Village and I remember feeling silly asking the clerk if they had the book, like they would immediately know that I had just seen it on television. (I also remember thinking some of the trivia questions in the book weren't exactly fair, like the ones that asked when all the *Star Wars* actors' birthdays were.)

A lot went on between third and sixth grade, mostly forming a John Hughes-worthy blueprint for dorkdom: I got glasses, watched my best friend move away, learned to play the clarinet (never very well), co-wrote my first long story (15 pages! With pictures!), finally read all the way through "The Lord of the Rings," started noticing girls for real, started being ignored by girls for real, and made it to a regional spelling bee.

In a weird way, I now kind of realize that having been the perfect age – six – when *Star Wars* came out, I was also at the perfect age for the saga to be closing. By spring of sixth grade, I was pretty much too old for Kenner's toys, and let's face it: The prospect of keeping up a teenage *Star Wars* fan-face in the social meat-grinder of junior high? No thanks.

At the same time, though, I was still a 12-year-old boy, so lightsabers and spaceships and stormtroopers remained fun ideas, and if you're going to put Princess Leia in a metal bikini: Again, perfect age for it.

I don't remember what movie I went to see at the Gold Circle Cinemas the night I first saw the *Return of the Jedi* trailer. Heck, I can't even honestly remember if I saw the fabled original *Revenge of the Jedi* version. I do remember telling all my friends about it (we were almost all still *Star Wars* fans on some level, though I feel confident in saying nobody had it as bad as I did), and specifically talking about the shot of Chewbacca picking up a stormtrooper and throwing him backwards into another trooper, which seemed to me the very definition of "awesome."

So now it's late May 1983, and *Jedi* is set to open.

On a freaking Wednesday night.

Arggh! That's a *school* night, George! What are you *thinking*?! I can't go to see a movie on a *school night*! You're killing me!

Did I ask my parents a few days beforehand? I honestly don't know. If I did, they hadn't given me a concrete answer, because otherwise I'd remember bragging at school about going.

I got home from school around 3:30, and the pestering began. "Can we, Mom? Dad? Please? Can Mike" – this would be Mike S. – "come along if we go? CanweCanweCanwe?"

Sweet God, they said YES! Mom, Dad, my little brothers Nick and Adam and I piled into our Ford conversion van, drove up to Hartville and picked up Mike and then headed down to Canton to Mellett Mall.

I seem to think we got to the mall around 5 o'clock for something like an 8 o'clock showing.

Pulling into the parking lot, nothing seemed out of the ordinary. Mellett Mall's Twin Cinemas' only entrance was from inside the shopping center, so the giant movie marquee outside hung on a big plain brown brick wall. No flashing lights, no mass of fans gathering in front of the theater. Just *Return of the Jedi* in big plastic, all-capital letters. Remembering what it was like to see that sign still tightens my chest a little bit.

When we went inside it was quickly clear this was not an ordinary night at the movies. A line, two and three people wide, led from the theater's entrance out past the novelty T-shirt shop next door, past Casual Corner and the Little Professor Bookstore and on down the concourse toward Montgomery Ward. I'd never seen a line like this outside of Cedar Point or Disney World.

And there was an energy to it. Not the kind like we saw in the prequel era, when people came out in costumes and you'd see fully-armored Stormtroopers and robed Jedi and maybe a Boba Fett or four, but just an anticipatory thrill, everybody talking and excited and ready to find out how this whole thing was going to end up. (Did we know it was going to be the wrap-up to the saga? I can't imagine otherwise, but then, I can't exactly recall thinking that I was going to see the last *Star Wars* movie ever, either.)

So, here we were. Hyper. Frantic. Psyched.

And facing a three-hour wait until showtime.

No advance ticket sales here, this was good old-fashioned get in line, tickets go on sale maybe an hour, tops, before a showing, wait your turn and have a friend hold your spot if you have to pee.

Mom, Dad, Nick, Adam, Mike and I parked ourselves at the end. (People piled in behind us pretty steadily, so we weren't at the end long.) Mike and I ran up to the front of the line to look at the movie posters and the accompanying photos in their lit-up glass frame, pointing and wondering and yammering about how cool this was and how great it was to be there.

We ate dinner in two shifts: Clutching some money from Mom and Dad, we ran down to the hot dog shop – it might have been called "Carousel" – and the Orange Julius next door. (That was, I'm pretty sure, all the food choices Mellett Mall had to offer. Food courts wouldn't reach Canton for another few years.) It felt neat, being 12 years old and kind of on our own. Sure, my family was right down the mall, but these were pre-cell phone days, and there was a sort of freedom in the air as we ordered our own food, found a place to sit, talking and joking while we ate our hot dogs and Orange Julius.

Then we held the spot in line when Mom and Dad took my little brothers for dinner.

It's funny how much of the next few hours I *don't* remember from that May evening in 1983.

I don't remember the line eventually creeping forward, or the moment our tickets came spitting up through the little slot in the counter, or finding our seats, or the lights going down, or the previews.

I don't remember the tense anticipation brought on by the 20th Century Fox fanfare or the chills on the back of my neck at the blast of sound when the *Star Wars* logo slammed onto the screen.

What I really remember is a feeling.

I've never seen a movie in an atmosphere like that again. Packed houses on opening nights with hardcore fans, sure, but never again like this one.

We were *there*.

All of us were there in the Tatooine desert, screaming and whooping when Artoo launched Luke's lightsaber through the hot, wavering air. We were in the cramped, firelit hut when Yoda confirmed Vader's secret. Yes, we even joined the Ewoks' battle cries, feeling the ground shake under the thundering fall of an Imperial Scout Walker.

God, I was so excited to go to school the next day, because this time, it was me who'd gotten to go see the next *Star Wars* movie first, and I couldn't wait to talk about it and see if anyone else had been to opening night. Funny thing is, nobody had. Not only that, nobody seemed as caught up in the whole thing, at least, not the way they'd been a couple years before about *Empire*. Guess that's what three years, especially those between third and sixth grade, will do.

Somewhere in the years after *Jedi*, it became cool to sell the movie short, mostly because of the Ewoks, but also because of the whole Luke/Leia-brother/sister coincidence, and the flip dialogue and the re-hashing of the Death Star battle. And even though a lot of us first-generation fans recognize those things, I'd bet very few of us felt that way right after seeing it. Weakest of the original trilogy? No doubt – but I don't remember a single person coming out of that theater saying the Ewoks sucked or that they felt ripped off or that Lucas had gotten lazy.

Because what I remember most vividly about that night is the moment of triumph when Vader is turned at the last, swooping the Emperor up in those armored arms as John Williams' score assaulted our ears. A wave of awestruck adrenaline rushed through the theater, and the audience actually stood in unison and cheered, caught up in the climax. I've never seen that happen at any other movie screening.

That's my favorite movie scene ever. Even a quarter-century and a thousand watches later, it still manages to spark whatever cells hold the faintly-vibrating echoes of that night. For the shortest of blinks, things around me go dark, and I taste hot dogs and Orange Julius and popcorn and Coke and then my throat and guts do a Jell-O shiver and Mom and Dad and Nick and Adam and Mike are there beside me and we're in a crowd that's wide-eyed and applauding and grinning in the movie screen's flicker.

It always passes more quickly than I hope, but as long as those seconds still happen, somewhere I still get to be twelve.

Proof of Purchase

Mom bought me the *Return of the Jedi* comic paperback at Click's one afternoon not long after the movie came out. I had started reading it at the magazine racks by the checkout lanes and dove back into it as soon as we were in the car.

We only lived about 10 minutes from the store, but by the time we got home, I was already about halfway into the book, and I had this faint feeling of sadness that I hadn't slowed down to enjoy it more.

Although I'd already seen *Return of the Jedi*, I was visiting Jake in the summer of 1983 the first time he went to see it. This was after he'd moved away, remember, and it was great being in the theater with my *Star Wars* pal again, three years after the late-for-*Empire* afternoon. When Lando wheeled the Falcon over the Death Star's surface and dove into its maze of passages, I remember leaning over and saying to Jake, "Awww, yeah – one more time!"

It's Not My Fault

This essay began as an ever-growing list on a yellow legal pad under the header "Stuff I Watched Because of *Star Wars*."

Should've added "or Read or Did or Thought Of" in there, too, because I can't think of a single science-fiction or space fantasy, future-seeing or rocket-fueled book or movie or TV show that I saw before the age of six.

After the summer of 1977?

Ate. It. Up.

Nothing touched *Star Wars*, but *Star Wars* touched everything.

Even movies or TV shows with actors from *Star Wars* in them were must-see stuff, sci-fi or not.

I watched *Force Ten from Navarone* every time it aired on Channel 43 out of Cleveland thinking it was awesome because Harrison Ford starred in it. Oddly enough, that kid Craig who was with me and Jake when we went to see *Empire* was over visiting one of those times.

I was eleven when *Blade Runner* came out and I was dying to see it because Han Solo looked like a badass and it was totally a science fiction movie with future cities and floating cars and stuff, and I remember my parents either seeing it or seeing a preview for it and my mom declaring, "Absolutely not."

I had to settle for owning an orange Matchbox version of Deckard's car with the movie logo stamped on it.

I wouldn't see *Blade Runner* until my freshman year of college, when my friend Jen was watching it in one of her classes and asked if I wanted to come along. The prof was showing it on a TV with muddy sound, and we were in a really old, echo-y building, so honestly, I think I dozed through large chunks of it because the dialogue was lost in the Vangelis soundtrack. I loved it anyway.

There was *Corvette Summer,* watched on TV and starring Mark Hamill. I must've seen this with a babysitter or something, because I can't imagine my parents letting me sit through this movie about a high school kid and his new hooker friend tracking down his stolen car.

American Graffiti, naturally – I fell in love with this movie long before I had any business doing so.

Little Lord Fauntleroy with Alec Guinness. Ugh. I tried, Obi-Wan, I tried. Ten minutes and I was bored to tears. (Sir Alec made up for it years later when I finally got around to watching *The Bridge on the River Kwai.*)

Just after my family got our first VCR (complete with our first remote control, which was – wait for it – *attached to the VCR by a long cord*), Mom picked up some movies from a place where you could *rent them and watch them at home!* Oh. My. God. How. COOL.

I kid you not: This store was, literally, the refurbished living room of someone's house. I mean, it was clearly a home-business setup – there were video racks and movie posters and a cash register and everything, and it wasn't like there were couches in there – but you still went in through the front porch.

Mom had brought me a movie called *Destination: Moonbase Alpha.* It's goofy and ridiculous in retrospect, but at the time, it was a space movie, and that was good enough for me.

Same sort of memory when Roger Corman's *Battle Beyond the Stars* was shown on TV – wow, this was silly stuff, and a little embarrassing when the characters started talking about alien sex, but the formula held: John + space movie = kid enthralled.

I made a point of watching *The Martian Chronicles* miniseries long before I discovered Ray Bradbury for real, but I missed the middle episode where everyone on Mars watches Earth erupt in nuclear fire. I don't think it would've made a difference, though: The only scene that sticks with me is the end of the series, where Rock Hudson and his family go to see the Martians and he takes them to see their own reflections in a river.

I'm fairly certain I didn't get it.

Confession: I still like *The Black Hole,* Disney's attempt at jumping on the *Star Wars* Bantha-wagon. The commercials showing the flat plane of space as a green-on-black vector grid stretched obscenely by a whirlpoolish pit gave me the kind of creepy stomach butterflies I still get from heights occasionally.

Visually, it wasn't *Star Wars,* but *The Black Hole* had some cool things going for it: The hole itself, for starters, massive and slowly rotating, its menacing maw in the background; the double-barrelled hand blasters; the spooky lobotomized human zombies in their mirrored masks and dark robes; the devil robot Maximilian and his shred-o-matic attack blades. (Pretty vicious for a Disney flick, but then, you never really saw anyone get their chest turned into coleslaw – it was way more about the suggestion than the event. When we played *Black Hole* on the playground after seeing the movie, everybody relished their turn at being Maximilian.) Then there was the Cygnus – the ghost ship teetering on the edge of the black hole itself. I remember Dad telling me he thought this was a pretty cool ship, with its old-time feel of decay and antiquity, and its exposed girders and expanses of glass.

Oh, man, there was *Krull,* and believe it or not, Jake and I saw this on one of my visits to Cincinnati and we freaking loved it. Clearly, I'd caught some kind of "bad sci-fi is still sci-fi" virus.

On TV, there were new-to-me episodes of the old "Lost in Space" series in those kid-friendly after-school hours from 3 to 5 p.m., along with my first taste of Japanese cartoons: "Battle of the Planets."

Mornings, I'd get up early to catch the Japanese serial cartoon "Star Blazers," another role-playing inspiration for Jake and me. The idea of this old World War II battleship converted to a spacefaring machine with its "wave motion engine" kicking ass from the back and the gaping "wave motion gun" roaring from the bow was just tons of fun. (And though Jake swore he saw an episode where the female lead, Nova, had her uniform tear, exposing her cartoon boob, I missed that one and wasn't sure I believed him.)

Mike D. and his parents took me to see the Gil Gerard/Erin Gray *Buck Rogers in the 25ᵗʰ Century* movie, and I naturally got hooked on the TV show it launched, but nothing on the small screen came close to touching *Battlestar Galactica*.

Cylons and their never-ending *whoom-whooming* red eyes and the Vader-esque grill where their mouths should be, and the emotionless and chilling "By your command" repeated endlessly? Freakshow good.

Vipers and launch tubes and cold-blooded Cylon Raiders and Basestars and the Galactica herself, who looked like some kind of snake-headed alien machine creature on the attack.

Seriously – this crap was awesome. The episode where they go up against a guy who's apparently the incarnation of Satan scared the bejeezus out of me, and the two-parter with Lloyd Bridges and Galactica's long-lost sister Battlestar Pegasus holds up, I swear, loaded with cheese as it is.

I started seeking out sci-fi books, too. Uncle Rob, having sown seeds of nerd-dom with the *Lord of the Rings* books, gave me a non-fiction Isaac Asimov paperback about space and time and the universe that just blew my mind and led me to his short stories. And I'm pretty sure my old first edition of Robert Silverberg's "Revolt on Alpha C" came from Uncle Rob's boyhood bookshelf.

There was "Dar Tellum, Stranger from a Distant Planet" and "A Wrinkle in Time" and its sequels and the abridged kid-ified versions of "20,000 Leagues Under the Sea" and "War of the Worlds" and "The Time Machine."

Once, when I was in the Waldenbooks at the mall looking through the science-fiction shelves with a gift certificate burning a hole in my pocket, a guy browsing nearby recommended Frederick Pohl's "Gateway." I read the blurb on the back: Long-dead alien civilizations, space trips to forgotten planets – sounded like my kind of thing.

Only it wasn't: It was conversations with a psychoanalysis computer and sex talk and people learning how to flush complicated rocket toilets. And I remember awkwardly telling my parents, when they asked how it was, that it was OK. It had the f-word in it, though, I confessed, and I never managed to make it through, even though I know now that it's a sci-fi classic.

In fifth grade, my friend Mike S. and I wrote a 15-page interplanetary adventure, "The Creanaz Syndrome," about a couple kids on horseback getting abducted by aliens. The origin was a box of "story starter" cards in Mrs. Tomits' classroom that gave you a couple paragraphs by way of introduction, and then you were supposed to conclude the story. Mike and I picked one that began with a girl – Joan, I think – wondering where her friend Rick had disappeared to during their short horse-trail trek. From there – BOOM! – aliens. (I told Mike I could take any plot device and use it as the basis for an outer-space story. "Archaeology," he challenged me. Piece of cake, I responded. You dig up something in the desert or wherever, and it turns out to be from another planet. Obvious as it seemed, this felt like a particularly cool notion at the time, since we were in fifth grade and we hadn't seen or heard that idea a billion times yet.)

It wasn't just fictional outer-space stuff that hooked me either: I started subscribing to "Odyssey," an astronomy and space magazine for kids. Home, in fact, to my first published work: A two- or three-paragraph story based on seeing the image of Cleveland Indians mascot Chief Wahoo in the moon.

I couldn't get enough of space shuttle coverage when NASA launched the program in 1981; at sixth-grade camp, I remember being to scared to ask this girl Denise to dance, and then going outside to look at the rings of Saturn through the science teacher's telescope.

Even in my twenties when I lived in Orlando, I took every possible opportunity to drive out and watch shuttle launches from Cape Canaveral, and they never stopped giving me goosebumps.

Star Wars helped make me a bit of a geek.

I've learned to live with it.

Proof of Purchase

As a kid, I wrote fan letters to Harrison Ford and Carrie Fisher, both care of Del Rey Books, publishers of the *Star Wars* novels and the spin-offs. Long after I forgot I'd sent those letters, I received autographed 5-by-7 black-and-white photographs in the mail.

Harrison's was in marker, so I couldn't really tell if it was a stamp or the real thing, but Carrie's was in ballpoint, and you could see the imprint on the picture.

I lost the Harrison picture, but still have Carrie's and the autograph seems to match up to the ones I've seen from public signings she's done.

Being twelve and getting a signed picture of Princess Leia in the Jabba's Palace Slave Girl outfit? Cool. Sharing it with your parents when they ask, "What was in that letter today?" Squirmy.

Perfect Hibernation:
The Lean Years

I'm lucky to have two brothers who are seven and eight years younger than me.

Lucky because it meant I got *Star Wars* all to myself during the early years, and lucky again because later on, when I was supposed to be outgrowing my *Star Wars* toy addiction – say, the last year before *Return of the Jedi* came out in 1983 – Nick and Adam had grown into *Star Wars* territory, so the pipeline from Kenner to our basement never went dry. Though they both moved on to Transformers and Micro Machines and other stuff after the *Star Wars* phenomenon faded, it's thanks to them that I have some of the later toys like the Ewok Village Playset and the Imperial Shuttle and the Speeder Bikes and the B-Wing and Jabba the Hutt.

The last Kenner toy I specifically asked for was the Y-Wing, and I remember Mom giving me a "Really? Aren't you a little old for that?" kind of look. Might have even been a direct question.

Maybe so. After all, the Y-Wing came out around the same time *Jedi* did, so I was 12 years old turning 13 when I asked for it. Couldn't help it. This thing was light years ahead of the old X-Wing, and armed with not only that squealing laser cannon, but a rotating top turret and a plastic bomb to drop from its underbelly, and a socket behind the cockpit for Artoo units. I may not have actually role-played with my figures anymore, but I did send that ship on many a run over card houses built in our living room, and somewhere in our family albums there's a snapshot of me using the ship to dive-bomb Adam and his *Knight Rider*-inspired remote-control black Camaro.

Growing out of *Star Wars* was happening all around me. Mike D. and I weren't close friends anymore, my other *Star Wars*-obsessed pal, Jacob, had moved down to Cincinnati, and after the final chapter of the saga came out, things just seemed to quiet down.

I kept my fandom mostly low-key in those years, breaking out only the occasional quote among close friends.

In seventh grade, the Scholastic book order form that was delivered to our English class once a month included the *Return of the Jedi* Sketchbook. I placed my order for it, only to have my money returned a week or so later when the teacher told me that the class hadn't met the minimum order amount. I think I responded with something along the lines that my birthday was coming up anyway, so no big deal.

"And," she told me in what was supposed to be a consolatory tone but instead just sounded incredibly condescending, "maybe you'll be over your *Jedi* phase by then." I did, in fact, get a five-dollar Waldenbooks gift certificate for my birthday that year, and I did go to Belden Village and use it to buy that sketchbook. *Jedi* phase, indeed.

Still, for most of middle school and high school, my *Star Wars* bug was kind of holed up, nearly dormant, nibbling on the occasional scrap that fell its way. A girl I dated when I was 16, for instance, had a dad who was an executive at a record store chain, and in her basement, in a box of discarded record albums, I found the *Return of the Jedi* soundtrack, which she gave to me. And when the local newspaper ran an Associated Press story headlined "'Star Wars' still with us after 10 years," I clipped it out and saved it. (Yes, I still have them both.)

Literally and metaphorically, the *Star Wars* habit went into the closet: My surviving toys were arranged as best I could fit them on the shelves in the walk-in I had in my bedroom: There was my original banged-up display for the first dozen action figures, and my small metal Millennium Falcon, and a Tauntaun and my Landspeeder, which was now missing its top engine pod. I used that blue sticky-tack stuff to attach prints from the Star Wars Portfolio to the wall, along with a collage I made by cutting up the photos from a bunch of my action figure packages and sticking them to what had been part of my Y-

Wing Box. (I also had a folding chair, a boom box, and an old television tray-table in there, where I'd sit and write with Mom's Smith-Corona typewriter while listening to cassette tapes.)

When I was in high school, I got a job at the Children's Palace down by the mall. For most of the 1980s, this was the toy store we begged our parents to take us to. At the time, it seemed absolutely monstrous – it had faux castle towers on its façade, which helped – because the only other toy stores were Kay-Bee Toys and Hobby Center in the mall, both of which seemed just plain pathetic when compared with Children's Palace and its acres of toys stretching impossibly high into a distantly buzzing haze of fluorescent lighting. I can remember when the place had its own *Star Wars* section, a canyon wall of black and silver packaging, that familiar logo reproduced into infinity. You'd stretch an arm back between rows of figures hanging on their pegs, craning your neck and pushing each toy aside just slightly to see the one behind it, looking for the one you didn't have.

Later, when the toys were on clearance, I found a huge pile of Rancor Monsters at the rear of the store, marked down to five bucks each, and I bought one to replace Nick and Adam's, which I'd broken an arm off of.

I worked nights and weekends, starting as a seasonal employee before Christmas of 1988, straightening merchandise, re-stocking shelves. I stayed part-time there for the next two or three years, mostly working the floor and spending some time in the warehouse, unloading trucks and pulling items like bicycles and swingsets for customers, who had to drive around the back of the building to pick up the big-ticket purchases.

I also spent time in the Peter Panda suit. Peter Panda was the corporate mascot, and once a month or so, someone was asked to put on the suit and spend a work shift wandering the aisles and either making kids smile or inadvertently scaring the shit out of them. The panda suit was a huge, padded thing, hot and heavy, but I liked volunteering to wear it. For one thing, it meant not having to interact with the customers, because Peter wasn't allowed to speak. No having to fake a smile, either, thanks to the one sewn onto the oversized panda face. (Though I have to admit, I smiled at about two hours' worth of little kids during my first time in the suit before I realized it was just wasted effort. In one of my later Panda stints, I stood largely motionless outside to promote a sidewalk sale and actually put on headphones and listened to Nine Inch Nails' *Pretty Hate Machine*.) Panda time also earned the wearer something like a 10-minute break for every 20 minutes on duty, which really made a four-hour weeknight shift fly past.

I even talked my bosses into letting me borrow the thing to wear to my then-girlfriend's high school graduation party, which was fun, especially driving over to her house wearing the body of the suit, with my huge, furry bear paw cocked nonchalantly out the window as I tried my best to work the gas and brake pedals while wearing costume tennis shoes with soles the size of turkey platters.

There wasn't a defined *Star Wars* section at Children's Palace anymore by the time I worked there – the big crazes during my tenure were *The Real Ghostbusters* and *Teenage Mutant Ninja Turtles* – but for awhile, there was still some *Star Wars* stuff to be found sulking on the clearance shelves and squirreled away in the piles of old merchandise on the shelf-tops. I remember pegs near floor level displaying *Return of the Jedi* badges and pencil cases, just above some Emperor's Royal Guard plastic banks. They were all as far away from the rest of the real toys as you could get, sandwiched between the baby bottles and teething rings and the bicycle department.

Using one of the big metal ladders – they were more like staircases on wheels – I fished around the stuff on top of the shelves in the action figure aisle and came up with a Chewbacca Bandolier, a Kenner Micro Death Star Compactor Playset, and a Laser Rifle Carry Case to hold action figures. (There was an Indiana Jones truck up there that I should've bought, too.) And during a warehouse shift, I was poking around in the loft up near the ceiling and found a big cardboard box with "C-3PO Cases" written in marker on the side. Inside was a single shiny-as-new action figure case. I was amazed to find that clearance prices for this stuff were still in the computer system: The Bandolier cost me 90 cents; the Micro Death Star $2.90, and the carrying cases were, I think, $1.90 each. And I either bought or swiped (sorry, CP executives) an Emperor's Royal Guard ink stamper and the Parker Brothers *Return of the Jedi* Play for Power card game.

Finding *Star Wars* merchandise was like unearthing a rare prize on an archaeological dig, but I still opened them up and threw away the packaging, which makes me wince a little now, but then I think that because I *did* open those toys, it means I still saw them at least partially through the eyes of that 7-year-old I had been when *Star*

Wars first came out. They were still toys to me, and not collectibles, and that's something I've tried to keep hold of.

I took all these things home and set them in my closet with the rest of my Kenner leftovers. The miniature-scale Death Star may have gotten a publicly-visible spot on one of my bookshelves, out of fondness for its long-deceased big brother. None of them is really a cool *Star Wars* toy: There's a reason they were on clearance and still gathering dust in Children's Palace several years after *Jedi*'s theatrical release. But I still have most of them, because they remind me of a time when *Star Wars* had left the public eye and was kind of a secret treasure.

Toys "R" Us later moved in right across the street and pretty quickly drive Children's Palace out of business.

I would be a college student at Bowling Green State University before interest in the original trilogy began its resurgence in bookstores and comic shops. "*Star Wars* is back," people started to whisper.

Some of us just brought our toys back out of the closet and smiled, knowing it had never left.

Proof of Purchase

In seventh grade Algebra, my friend Dave and I were fake-fighting over a pencil before class started, tugging at it from both ends.

"Mine!" I squawked in Yoda's voice. "Or I will help you not!"

Dark Times

When I was a freshman at Bowling Green State University, I went to my first Big Lots store. High on a shelf I found a whole stack of *Star Wars* record totes, sized to hold vinyl 45s. This was the fall of 1989, mind you, so grabbing one of these for 50 cents was a treat and a trip and many, many times since, I've realized that I should have gone back with a five-spot and bought a pile of them. I used it to collect my pens and pencils and desk clutter and that's what it's still for almost two decades later.

It was a good farewell to the '80s and a great way to start the '90s, stretching myself out in the flatlands of northwest Ohio. Between the old and new friendships, regular fights and tears and ridiculous joy, I can't think of another time in my life where everything in every moment seemed to matter so much. It still feels very close and very real.

And yet within a few years, I'd made some stupid relationship decisions, alienated most of my friends and family, and moved a thousand miles away from everyone who mattered to me while my Dad was dying of cancer.

At the same time, there's a thread of *Star Wars* running through the whole period, particularly during the years I call (only half-jokingly) the "Dark Times."

The last good summer, 1991, my friend Ivan and I lived in a crappy, boxy apartment in BG to take summer classes and enjoy a little independence away from home. We had original *Star Wars* trilogy posters above the little black-and-white television set in the living room were we watched a lot of "Twilight Zone" and "Star Trek: The Next Generation."

That summer, my buddy Aaron came up for a day or two and told me about this book he'd started reading called "Heir to the Empire." Aaron had never been a big reader, so I knew this had to be something special. I was hooked immediately, and I remember lying on an overstuffed, worn blue couch underneath the sole window in the living room reading while the hot breath that passed for a summer breeze wafted faintly through the apartment. Ivan scarfed the book down as quickly as I did – I think we may have even read the same copy simultaneously, passing it back and forth as we came in and out of the house from classes, summer jobs and WBGU radio duties.

I had a brown and tan bathrobe that had been Dad's when I was growing up and which I'd used as an Obi-Wan getup on a trip to Ohio University for Halloween a few years before. (Back before the days of the 501st and online costuming groups, a white bedsheet toga, a brown turtleneck and brown beach towel hood plus that robe and a flashlight made for a perfectly passable Jedi outfit.)

Every so often, post-shower or in the morning, or whenever, I'd be wearing this robe around the apartment, and if Ivan passed through the room, I'd throw out a random Obi-Wan quote: "The Jundland Wastes are not to be traveled lightly."

"…and no questions asked."

"Many of the truths we cling to…"

Walking from the bathroom across the hall to my room once, I caught a glimpse of Ivan sitting in the living room and, without stopping, said, "Run, Luke, run!"

Ivan objected, insisting that this was Obi-Wan's spirit voice, and not eligible for inclusion in the Robe Dialogues. I responded that since I hadn't spoken before passing out of Ivan's line of sight that the quote was valid.

Man, I wish I still had things that important to discuss on a summer morning.

I had never stopped being a *Star Wars* fan, but in the post-*Jedi* years, I explored different (though still largely nerdy) paths: I discovered Ray Bradbury in the BGSU library stacks and read every collection and novel I could get my hands on. I'd played games like Archon and Infocom's text adventures incessantly on our Commodore 64 in high school, and I'd toyed with role-playing Dungeons & Dragons and later Shadowrun. I did college radio comedy and got my FCC permit to host. They Might Be Giants and REM and New Order and the Pet Shop Boys and Mannheim Steamroller (well before they built their Christmas-schmaltz empire) were my soundtrack.

On a spring break trip to Florida my sophomore year, I rode Star Tours for the first time. My friend Adam, whom I'd known since fourth grade, worked at one of the Disney resorts and got me and our friend Mike in for five days straight on passes. It rocked, seeing the ride and the giant AT-AT and the fake Ewok village and the prop sand skiff and snowspeeder at what was then called the Disney-MGM Studios.

While I was there, I bought an Imperial Walker T-shirt that was my favorite ever.

So when Aaron brought me that Timothy Zahn book, long after our sequel-writing and *Star Wars* RPG-collecting days had faded, I was psyched like I hadn't been in a long time. A long time.

Like I said, I'd never stopped being a *Star Wars* fan, but that book, that summer, was like hooking the jumper cables to the Landspeeder up on blocks in the back yard.

By the time that summer came to a close, I was dating the girl who'd wind up helping me make an emotional wreck of myself over the next few years, though the real shitty times were a little ways off yet. On the bright side, though, I had *Star Wars* actively back on the brain.

When summer 1992 rolled around, my life was very different. During the previous school year, That Girl had moved into my room in the new apartment Ivan and I were sharing. This pissed off my parents and widened the gap between me and my closest friends because That Girl found extreme fault with most of them and was a bitch anytime someone I cared about came near. Blind, I was. And stupid. And stubborn.

Ivan moved away after the first semester, subletting his room to a guy I didn't know.

Dad's cancer came back. He'd had a kidney removed during my senior year of high school, but we hadn't seen signs of the illness since. It was hitting his lymph nodes now. He and Mom asked me to come home for the summer. That Girl begged me to stay in Bowling Green.

I decided to compromise and go back and forth every two or three weeks, but was a spineless asshole and spent most of that summer in BG, back in the boxy, cramped apartment that had been such a cool and fun place just a year before.

Bit by bit, the pieces of my life moved from the house where I grew up into that apartment: my books, my posters, my pictures. My *stuff*.

My *Star Wars* guys.

Once, my wife Jenn asked me about the good times I'd had with That Girl. I know they were there, and I may have even come up with one, but they feel fake and only justified afterwards, even though at the time they felt genuine.

The gradual comeback of *Star Wars* is now pretty much the only good stuff I remember coming out of my two years on the Dark Side, from late 1991 until November or so of 1993.

Living with each other, That Girl and I fought a lot. She latched onto my love for *Star Wars* and fueled it, which you'd think would be cool, but turned out to be just another way to manipulate me.

Still, this was the time when neat stuff was happening: Zahn's book had re-stoked the *Star Wars* fires, and I was itching for his sequel.

Then Steve Sansweet's "*Star Wars*: From Concept to Screen to Collectible" book came out. This thing came at me out of nowhere one afternoon in a mall bookstore, and I absolutely devoured it: page after page of the toys I'd had, the toys I'd craved, and sweet God, the toys I'd never even known existed but now wanted to see. And for just the second time in my life, my eyes fell upon the image of a Blue Snaggletooth. This single picture and one-paragraph explanation of the figure's existence, maybe more than anything else in that book, put the scent of *Star Wars* collecting back in my nostrils. "Collecting" even seems too antiseptic and grown-up. This nostalgia was like being little again and feeling that bone-deep desire to Collect All 21!

There was only one comic shop in Bowling Green, but I figured they might have some of the old Marvel books I remembered, so I paid a visit.

And I got another smack upside the head: The *Star Wars* comics from my childhood were there in the longboxes, of course, but ... there were also *new Star Wars* comics on the racks!!!

That's how I stumbled onto Dark Horse's "Dark Empire" and "Classic *Star Wars*" comics.

Suddenly I had new Zahn books *and* new comics to wait for, and I had old stuff to hunt for.

I started seeking out comic shops and old toy dealers up in Toledo just to see what vintage *Star Wars* things they might have around. Because this was pre-Internet, you could still discover things in the real world because everybody and their mom didn't think a chewed-up Vader from the sandbox was worth a box of gold.

I loved these places. I loved seeing *Star Wars* figures still on their cards and ships still in their boxes. I loved seeing things I hadn't as a kid, like the Desert Skiff and the electronic Laser Battle and Battle Command games. I remember seeing my first vintage fan-custom figure: a Slave Leia (shock!) sitting near the cash register in one of these places.

My favorite stop was a comic store in a strip mall in Toledo run by a guy who was the closest I could imagine to a real-life version of Doc Brown from *Back to the Future*. He wore a long trenchcoat all the time and was kind of wild-eyed and messy-haired and flapped around the store excitedly looking for stuff among the piles of seemingly disorganized boxes. He'd point me to a crate or a corner and I'd start rummaging. This is where I got stuff like my original *Star Wars* movie theater program and the January 1978 "Mad" magazine with Alfred E. Neuman as Vader on the cover and old fanzines and weird publications with titles like "Enterprise" and "Star Quest Comix."

I replaced the original six-issue Marvel *Star Wars* comic books I'd long since read into dust, then the six issues or so that followed, and then I added more when I could.

I found all four Burger King *Return of the Jedi* glasses at a local flea market one Saturday morning and picked up the lot for two bucks.

I brought all my original *Star Wars* guys to the apartment and set them up on a drawing board in the corner of the living room, and if there'd been room for the ships, they'd have been there, too.

At a card show in a Toledo mall, I bought the entire set of red-bordered Topps *Return of the Jedi* cards I had as a kid. Here, I also discovered the blue-bordered *Jedi* set I had never even known existed, and the gold-bordered set of *The Empire Strikes Back* cards.

On a trip home to North Canton, I found some still-packaged "giant" Topps *Empire* cards at the Hartville Flea Market, yet something else I'd never seen.

It was kind of a second Golden Age for me, *Star Wars*-wise, and it was gorgeous and sustaining in its own way, because the rest of my life pretty much sucked hard.

Remember that plan to spend alternating two-week-periods at home with my family and my sick Dad? Yeah, That Girl made that impossible with her guilt trips and needy emotional manipulation.

The one visit I remember making back to North Canton, That Girl and Ivan showed up. (Ivan was either back in Bowling Green for a visit or was planning his return to school there in the fall. I honestly don't remember.) They'd brought Ivan's car since That Girl was dependent on mine, and I'm pretty sure she also dragged him in to serve as kind of a buffer for the friction between her and my family. The one thing that stays in my mind is that the two of them had gone out and bought me a present: the new Timothy Zahn *Star Wars* book, "Dark Force Rising."

Fall 1992 was my last semester of college, and the sickening roller coaster ride continued.

Dad's cancer got worse. My closest friends and I grew more distant, since That Girl got along with none of them. I hardly spoke with my mom and my brothers. Life with That Girl was a series of fights and make-ups.

We bought and painstakingly assembled a *Star Wars* Millennium Falcon model together.

She shattered it against the wall one day during an argument.

She ripped my original trilogy posters down and shredded them in her hands.

This was how things went.

That Girl, in fact, said many horrible things and behaved terribly in many big and important ways, but maybe the thing that sums her up is this seemingly small act of pettiness: She would go out of her way to wear my Imperial Walker shirt by digging it out of my dresser or even the laundry and putting it on when I wasn't around. This way, see, I'd look like the selfish jerk if I took offense.

I didn't participate in my college graduation because she ridiculed the notion (having stopped taking classes herself). The day I should have been receiving my degree in front of my parents, I was working in the McDonald's where I'd met her, standing on an overturned plastic hamburger bun rack at the counter because the goddamn soda machine had exploded and there was an inch of pop on the floor.

In the spring of 1993, we moved to Orlando. I had my degree and wanted to do nothing more than find a job writing *anything*. That Girl wanted to live where it was warm, so we got jobs at McDonald's in Florida, working at different stores.

I said goodbye to my family and packed up most of my stuff on a quick overnight trip back home. Dad wasn't getting better. He and I both cried. I left anyway.

That Girl and I moved into another crappy apartment and ate a lot of cheap, bad food and scraped to pay our bills.

I displayed all my *Star Wars* figures and toys up on shelves in a closet and started looking for new shops to visit.

Mom and Dad and my brothers made their annual spring break trip to Madeira Beach on the Gulf Coast within a month or two of the move. They flew into Orlando, and I picked them up at the airport. Dad was wearing a chemo pump and looked frail and sallow. He slept in the apartment – That Girl was at work, thank God – while my mom and brothers and I walked around the neighborhood a little. They rented a car and drove over to Madeira for their vacation. Later that week, we went and visited them for a day, but of course, That Girl insisted on the two of us going out for lunch alone, even though we'd driven two hours to see my family.

At least I still had *Star Wars* to distract me.

Topps released its first set of "*Star Wars* Galaxy" trading cards, which I bought by the box until I completed a set. (Yes, we were still largely broke. I scrimped and tucked away dollars here and there so I could try to buy solace in *Star Wars* stuff.) I called about a half-dozen comic and card shops regularly in the lead-up to the release, asking when they'd be in.

A cool thing happened on my first visit to one of those shops in Orlando. I was talking with the owner about *Star Wars*, even though his was a more *Trek*-centric store called Enterprise 1701, and he ducked into a back room with a "hold on a sec" tossed over his shoulder. He came out with an old leftover admission ticket/flyer to an advance promotional screening of *The Empire Strikes Back*.

"Wow, that's pretty cool," I said, looking at it and then handing it back.

"Keep it," he said. "I have a whole stack of them."

It's still framed on my wall.

Even those ridiculous rubbery Galoob "Bend 'Ems" *Star Wars* figures were something to be had. Being in a store and seeing Stormtroopers and Vaders and Lukes hanging carded on the pegs was a rush, even if they were more like cruddy oversized erasers than "action figures."

I called my Dad on his birthday in early May. He sounded horrible. Not being able to afford a plane ticket, I boarded a Greyhound bus the next day and took a miserable 30-hour ride back to Ohio.

How miserable? Well, for reading material, I had "The Grapes of Wrath," and my entire travel provisions consisted of a box of sour-cream-and-onion snack chips, an Oscar Mayer packet of cheese, crackers and chicken slices, a Three Musketeers bar, a pudding cup, a package of M&Ms and a $1.19 in change. (Even this broke, I still plugged a quarter into a *Star Wars* arcade game at five in the morning at a stop in Louisville and blew up three Death Stars. Sometimes you just gotta let loose with the laser cannons.)

Dad was in really bad shape. When he spoke, it was weak and simple. Mom brought him a dish of his favorite ice cream, and he and I sat there in our living room while he ate it, and he looked up from a bite and said in this small, childlike voice, "I got spumoni."

One afternoon, he and I were sitting side-by-side on the couch looking out at the backyard. It was that golden time of day, the sun just starting to deepen with that light that made the green on the grass and the trees so rich. Bits of milkweed fluff drifted slowly and glinted over the fields and the yards. We weren't saying anything.

I was a thousand miles from That Girl, sleeping in the house where I grew up, looking out at the rows of towering pine trees Dad and I planted when I was about seven, and the tree fort on stilts we built with Rick and his dad.

And I felt like the real me for the first time in a long, long while.

I think my brothers and a couple of their friends were outside shooting hoops in the driveway.

After a few minutes, Dad turned to me and said, "Go play."

He died late one morning while I was out running errands.

My old friend Aaron came over. That night, he and my brothers and I watched the series finale of "The Wonder Years."

Despite my asking her to stay in Florida, That Girl came up for the funeral and managed to make things even shittier than they already were – a challenge, no doubt, but That Girl, she was more than up for it. Friends I thought I'd lost through my own bullheaded stupidity came to Dad's funeral, and I wanted to cry hard because even though I'd behaved beyond badly, they were here and God, I'd missed them.

But with That Girl back in town, the old me shriveled up to a husk and hid again, and the two of us left and went back to Orlando a day or two later.

Life went on.

We bought a computer at Sears, which I used mostly to play the X-Wing game, losing myself in the cockpit of a cheap barstool sitting at our kitchen counter.

The *Star Wars* Radio Drama was released, and I was an immediate fan for life.

Another store that had become one of my regular stops hosted Dave Prowse, the original guy in the Darth Vader suit, for an autograph signing one afternoon. (This was well before *Star Wars* celebs were making regular appearances anywhere. He drove up in his own rental car, got out his own box of stuff and walked in just like a regular guy.) Five bucks got me his signature on a trading card and a photo of us sitting side-by-side at the card table where he was signing. It was just about the coolest thing ever, and I even managed to wear my Imperial Walker shirt.

I bought a longbox for my comic books and customized it into a *Star Wars* vault. I walked to the nearby branch of the Orange County Public Library one day with a handful of change and a stack of *Star Wars* comics, book covers, record sleeves and other stuff and spent a while making black-and-white copies. At home, with magic markers, I added highlights to some of the images, then glued them all over the comic box and the lid and covered it all with contact paper.

I had one friend during this time whom I refused to let That Girl push me into excising from my life. She still lived in Ohio, but in late summer, 1993, she was in Florida to visit some friends she'd worked with one semester at Disney – she had sent me a C-3PO shirt my sophomore year of college because she said I used to remind her of him – and we spent a day together, That Girl-free. She stopped by the apartment and I remember showing her my closet-and-dresser-top display of *Star Wars* stuff and the lid to the comic box, which was all I had done at the time. It made her smile.

I hold tight to the memory of standing in the back room of that apartment, white walls and burgundy carpet and a sliding glass door letting sunlight pour in, along with the rest of that afternoon, because she died less than a year later, and that day was the last time I saw her alive.

The comic box has proven durable: It saw the end of the Dark Times, two apartments, a storage unit, a duplex, and three houses, and it still sits here beside my desk.

In the last months of that year, I finally broke up with That Girl and she moved out, and I blinked a lot as the world slowly brightened.

I had gotten a second job working as a tour guide at the Disney-MGM Studios, so I got to spend a lot of spare time hanging around Walt Disney World and riding Star Tours a ridiculous number of times. (I had a scheme to steal one of those orange flight suit Star Tours uniforms once, but never had the guts to pull it off, even though it totally would have worked.) The gift shop at the end of the ride sold tons of *Star Wars* loot, and during a weekend when cast members – this is how Disney refers to employees – got an extra discount on top of our normal one, I picked up a long-coveted three-volume signed and hardbound set of the complete Star Wars comic strips that Archie Goodwin and Al Williamson had done for newspapers back in the '80s.

And that November, I met Jenn, the girl I'd marry a little more than three years later. I was working the grill at yet another McDonald's and she was an insanely cute manager running the back drive-thru window. Our first just-as-friends date was a dollar-theater showing of *Jurassic Park* on 15-minutes' notice, and even though we didn't so much as hold hands that night, the Dark Times officially came to a close.

They were only two years, but even almost two decades later I still feel like I'm ripping off a scab when I remember how I treated my friends and family. When you're in your early twenties, it seems like every choice you make is an amplified earsplitting shout, every emotion a spiked lightning bolt, every tenuous bond a grip that will gash and scar when broken. Only later do you realize how quiet everything was to the rest of the world.

Everybody's got their Dagobah cave, I suppose.

Instead of seeing my face in Vader's helmet, I ran into That Girl in an Imperial Walker shirt.

The Future, the Past, and Old Friends:
The *Special Editions*

SWSE.mov.

That's the file, and it's taking for-freaking-EVER to download.

It's late 1996, and I'm sitting in the office/toy room of the two-bedroom apartment in Altamonte Springs, Florida, where Jenn and I live. My IBM PS/2 and its 486 processor and my newly-self-installed 24,800 baud modem are rattling and clanking their way through this then-massive two-megabyte download.

While waiting, I have cooked and eaten dinner and cleaned up and this thing is *still* loading.

It's dark outside, and Jenn's at work until 9 o'clock tonight.

From the three shelves mounted on the wall brackets above one end of my "computer desk" – it's a six-foot work table from Home Depot – a few dozen old and new *Star Wars* guys and ships keep me company.

*Whirrrr. Whirrrrrrrrrrr*buzz*whirr.*

It finishes. I close up Netscape and open QuickTime. My hands are shaking at the keyboard.

Within the small frame: darkness, unblemished.

Then the soft but powerful strains of a score, familiar and haunting, and there is a tightening in my chest. A television appears in the movie player, a tiny, boxed-in Star Destroyer chasing a still-smaller Rebel Blockade Runner, and a voice-over, tinny and pinched like water from a kinked hose reminds me that it's been an awfully long time since anyone's seen *Star Wars* anyplace besides television.

My entire body is goosebumps and my scalp is tingling and tense, and OhMyGodThisIsSoFreakingAWESOME, and then the music explodes and an X-Wing soars *out of the television screen and all the way into the camera's point of view* and the scene fills the frame and I think I just peed my pants.

Two minutes later, I watch it again. And again. And amen-freaking-again.

And when Jenn gets home, I'm pestering *her* to watch it the second she's in the door.

Because *Star Wars* is coming back to the big screen.

Hell, yes, I was excited. That little blurred and blocky movie file was adrenaline joy and hypertastic whoopage like nothing I'd known in years. I watched it daily for weeks.

Think of it: *Star Wars*. In a *movie theater*.

I don't care how many times you've seen it or how big your TV is or how ear-rippingly impressive your home sound system is, nothing touches *Star Wars* on the big screen. The darkness of a massive theater is somehow deepened by the projected blackness of space, then gingerly touched by the blue glowing words "A long time ago..." and then shattered by the sunburst of John Williams' opening *Star Wars* trumpets.

And it was coming back.

The glimpses we got of the computer-generated additions were, at the time, cool. (We'll nitpick them later. For now, we're still too giddy.) Seeing Jabba – even that goofy-looking version – talking with Han in Docking Bay 94 was neat because it felt like a nod to all us die-hards who remembered that scene from the novel and the comics. Newly-packed streets of Mos Eisley? Sweet. Sharper X-Wings in a camera flyby? Awe. Some.

My friend Mindé, who I used to work with at Disney's Backstage Studio Tour, had a second job working in a local strip mall movieplex, and when the *Star Wars* Special Edition teaser hit, she let me know what film it was attached to so we could go see it. And that's how I lost two hours of my life watching *Space Jam*. (It wasn't a solid two hours, at least: Halfway through the movie, when the next *Space Jam* was starting in the theater next door, we ducked out to go watch the *Star Wars* trailer again.)

Rumor was, after a time, that the trailer would be on the *Independence Day* videocassette when it came out. It wasn't.

The hype over the Special Editions built as January 1997 got closer.

By this time, I was working in the composing room of The Orlando Sentinel newspaper, and I watched the Arts & Entertainment pages religiously for updates on the project. When they ran a section-front article on the revamped trilogy, I asked for an extra printout of the page and its full-color overlay. I pulled extra copies of the ads we were pasting on the pages and took them home. Still have them, too.

Mindé got me one of the big teaser posters for the trilogy – the double-sided kind made to be displayed in a backlit frame – that had the 'awwww, yeah'-inducing tagline: "Three Reasons Why They Build Movie Theatres."

We ordered our opening night tickets for *Star Wars* about a month ahead of time, I think. About six or eight of us met up to see it at Downtown Disney, home of what were then the biggest and loudest movie theaters in central Florida.

The place was packed. I thought of *Jedi* opening night, except this time, there were handfuls of people in Stormtrooper armor and Jedi robes, and at least one paunchy Trekkie in a mustard-yellow Starfleet uniform.

The lights dimmed, and I squeezed my wife's hand, and then … we were watching *Star Wars*.

It was awfully loud, I remember, and Jenn says that Kelsey, still more than two months from joining us in the outside world, was kicking during the main theme.

What I also remember is watching that movie like I hadn't in a long time: eyes wide and darting across the screen trying to take everything in, wondering every few minutes if I was seeing something new or just re-noticing things I hadn't really looked at in years.

Hell, even the Greedo-shooting-first thing didn't bug me much at the time – although it started doing so pretty soon after – because I was just so caught up in the whole experience.

When *Empire* came out a few weeks later, Mindé got me and my friend Jim and my wife's little brother Andy into a late-night pre-screening. There were Trekkies in front of us in line scanning us with a fake tricorder. Honestly.

Jedi soon followed, and I saw it at another employee preview. This was one night after my Sentinel shift, which ended at 1:15 a.m. One of the temps I worked with was a kid named Jay who also worked at the mall cinemas down the street, and he said we could get into a showing that was supposed to start after the place was cleared and cleaned up from the last of the shows – about 1:15 or so.

We busted ass to hit the composing deadline and tore out of the Sentinel a few minutes early. Got to the theater with a couple minutes to spare.

And found the place looking locked down and empty.

It wasn't, of course, but looking through the front doors at the lobby and counter area, we saw everything cleaned and closed and not an employee in sight. They'd already wrapped things up and headed into the theater for their show.

Jay and I dashed around the back of the building to the appropriate exit door. We could hear the previews running and the sound system booming and people talking and laughing, and we banged on the door hoping someone would hear.

After about two minutes – long enough that I was ready to give up and head home – the door opened a crack and one of Jay's co-workers let us in. The place was surprisingly full, but we got our butts in a couple seats just as the previews ended.

Star Wars and *Empire* were still showing in a couple places, and there was one weekend where I desperately wanted to go see all three movies in a single day. It would have meant going to two different theaters practically across town, but it was possible. I don't remember why I didn't do it.

My daughter Kelsey was born in late March that year.

When she was six weeks old, I bundled her into her car seat/infant carrier, packed a couple bottles and diapers and baby stuff into a backpack, and drove to the one-dollar movie place where my wife and I had seen *Jurassic Park* on our first date. *Star Wars* was still showing back in the smallest theater. Maybe 70 seats, tops, and a sound system comparable to an eight-double-D battery boom box.

It was noon on a weekday. I think there may have been one other person there.

I sat in the back row on the right, put Kelsey's carrier on the seat next to me, and held her in the crook of my arm.

She probably slept through most of it. Never fussed or cried or squirmed.

But I looked down at her a lot during those couple hours – for some reason, I remember doing it during the Han/Jabba scene – and saw her little eyes wide open and glinting with the reflection of *Star Wars* on the screen.

Proof of Purchase

In 2005, while exploring the hotel room sales at *Star Wars* Celebration III in Indianapolis, I bought an original Han Solo action figure from Japan. Same figure as the Kenner version, but the beauty of vintage Japanese figure packaging was that it was just a little box, with the figure in a baggie inside. Nothing to tear open, nothing to ruin, and the small plastic bag had only been sealed with long-since-brittled tape.

For the first time in 20-some years, I opened a Kenner *Star Wars* guy.

Oh, sure, I'd gone through a phase of collecting Hasbro's remakes when they put them out in the mid-1990s. Hard not to get caught up in seeing *Star Wars* on the pegs and toy store shelves again, looking for figures I hadn't gotten yet, and wishing I could get all the ships. But as neat as it was seeing toys that hadn't existed when I was a kid – Luke's T-16 Skyhopper, a Grand Moff Tarkin figure – it didn't take long to tire of the hunt, and I realized I'd rather save my money and buy old *Star Wars* stuff.

So I opened this Han figure, and there was a whiff of brand-new plastic, just like when I tore into my Boba Fett and my Darth Vader and all the rest. The joints were squeaky tight, and the paint was still shiny, and suddenly things long gone didn't seem so far off at all.

Surrounding Us, Binding Us:
An Appreciation of the Prequel Era

Bad *Star Wars* is better than no *Star Wars*.

I found myself saying this a lot between 1999 and 2005.

A *lot*.

And I believe it, too. I really do.

Here's the thing, though: A big part of that is because the best memories I have of the Prequel Era aren't about the movies themselves. The joy was really in the anticipation and excitement and energy and sharing those things with my friends, family and fellow dorks.

Maybe it's because the original trilogy is too deeply ingrained in my psyche to be affected by what came after. Honestly: When I watch *Star Wars* and *Empire*, Darth Vader is as creepy and cold and straight-up terrifying evil has he ever was, because I've lived with that image for a lot longer than I've had to deal with the idea that it's just a grown-up whiny teen-angst Anakin in that suit.

So when I hear people moaning that these movies should never have been made, or read yet another online rant that "George Lucas raped my childhood," I kind of mentally shrug my shoulders and let it go, because I managed to have a lot of fun during those years, even if I did have to put up with all-too-conveniently hungry sea monsters and pointlessly-shapeshifting bounty hunters.

Part I: Every generation

I was working in the Sentinel's ad dummying department by the time the buzz was building over the first new *Star Wars* movie in 16 years.

I'd read a fair amount of speculation about the movie – my buddy Ivan and I once mailed each other copies of the *Entertainment Weekly* issue with an article about Ewan MacGregor as Obi-Wan, neither of us having any clue the other was chucking the same thing in the mail – but when it got closer, I decided to stay spoiler-free, limiting myself to the occasional sterile Lucasfilm-issued statement or picture.

Which means that by the time *The Phantom Menace* teaser trailer showed up online, I was hungry for it. I downloaded it onto my workstation the first chance I got, and it took me a bunch of tries because the connection kept timing out or locking up.

When the words "Every generation has a legend" appeared, I actually felt a lump in my throat. God, yes: Every generation – *my* generation – and this was *our* legend, returning to the big screen...

I watched it over and over and over. I downloaded a screensaver program that would play it silently on my desktop when I wasn't there, and I'd come back to find people hovering at my cubicle. The paper's movie writer asked how we could get the file up to his computer since it was too big to send through the office email system.

When they showed it on the local evening news, I videotaped it. I may not have known what to make of it, but I had the thing memorized within days.

My friend and co-worker Jim – also a lifelong *Star Wars* nut – and I talked about the trailer frame-by-frame: The odd-looking younger Yoda; Jedi knights blocking laser bolts left and right; the double-bladed lightsaber; this monstrous demon-looking guy whose red-and-black tattooed face I initially mistook for the burned visage of Darth Vader.

I was a little put off by this floppy-eared thing that made funny noises, but c'mon, how bad could it be? (*I know, I know.*)

When the second trailer came out and debuted on "The Today Show," I videotaped that one, too. And grabbed it for the work computer. And when my brother-in-law and I went to see *The Matrix*, we called ahead to make sure we were catching a showing with the *Episode I* preview attached.

That spring, Jim went to the first *Star Wars* Celebration in Denver. He said it was a rain-sopped, poorly-planned crowded mess – and he had a blast anyway, so I was jealous as hell.

In the mornings, Jenn left for work before I did. I'd get Kelsey ready to go to her grandma's and drop her off on my way in to the Sentinel. She was a little over a year old, and we made a habit of watching the two videotaped *Phantom Menace* trailers every day as we sat on the carpeted step between our dining room and our living room putting on our shoes.

One day, either before or after this little ritual, I quoted part of the trailer out loud to myself: "Wipe them out. All of them."

And my daughter, without hesitation, delivered the follow-up line: "Noooooooooooooo!"

It was gorgeous. Not even two yet and already quoting *Star Wars*. That moment alone is worth the price of the Prequel Era.

My job at the Sentinel at this point was to balance the needs of both the advertising and editorial departments and turn them into a layout for the newspaper. By a certain deadline, for instance, the editors would need to send me a guide of how much space they needed for stories, and the advertising sales reps would tell me how many ads they'd sold, and our department would put everything together like a puzzle.

Assembling the weekly entertainment section was one of my projects, and it was a doozy. Lots of ads, ranging from the big color ads for new movie openings to the one-column, one-inch plugs for dog racing and cheap ocean cruises, and lots of editorial listings that needed specific amounts of space laid out in specific formats.

Part of the gig, naturally, was dealing with salespeople who'd sell ads past deadline, meaning we'd have to find a way to shoehorn them in, since ads equal dollars. Some of the sales reps were regularly late with sizable color ads, but again, those meant bucks for the paper, so we gave them good-natured grief and made it work, and they'd buy us breakfast or lunch every so often.

I learned quickly that it paid off to be nice to the reps who handled movie ad accounts, and managed to get advance passes to stuff like *U.S. Marshals* and *James and the Giant Peach*.

Everybody knew I wanted *Phantom Menace* passes more than anything, especially Loreen, the rep who handled the 20th Century Fox account. She got her late color ads into the entertainment section without so much as a hint of an eye roll out of me.

One morning, I heard a co-worker taking a call from her. "Really?" he said. "Wow, thanks. That's pretty cool."

He hung up. "Hey John, guess what? Loreen just got me a couple *Star Wars* tickets!" Now, he was a very nice guy, and deserving of a night at the movies. Older than me, with a half-dozen kids, and an old-school nerd who reminisced about programming in COBOL and was a big *Star Trek* fan.

I tried to give him a genuine smile, and I must've failed miserably, because he just laughed and said, "No, she didn't. Just kidding."

As the numbers on my computer desktop's countdown clock to the *Episode I* opening got smaller, I asked Loreen regularly – but as casually as I could – about the possibility of scoring some passes. And I kept taking her late ads.

And I never got to see that countdown clock hit zero, because about three weeks before the movie opened, Loreen stopped by my desk with two tickets to an advance screening of the first new *Star Wars* movie in a generation. A couple days later, she even got me another one so I could get Jenn's little brother Andy in, too.

Man, was I ever psyched. The screening was in Altamonte Springs, a full 11 days before the official opening. When that evening finally arrived, we got to the theater about an hour and a half ahead of time, knowing there would be a line of other people who'd gotten tickets.

About a half-hour before we were let into the theater, I saw the guys from the Orlando-based boy band 'N Sync being shuttled out a side door into a waiting limo, presumably after a private screening. At least two of them were carrying plastic lightsabers. (The newer kind, not the original Kenner versions. Posers.)

The line moved forward. We handed over our passes, which bugged me, because I thought they could've just marked them or punched them or something so that we could keep the tickets themselves as a souvenir. When we went in and sat down, I was just overcome by this surreal feeling because there was going to be a *Star Wars* movie starting in a few minutes and I had no idea what to expect.

After that great rush of the 20th Century Fox fanfare and the opening theme and the giant familiar yellow *Star Wars* logo, the introductory crawl began, and things felt … weird. Oh, I was still excited, but it was a strange sensation to be seeing something new unfolding in that galaxy far, far away which to this point, I felt I knew like my own backyard.

In an odd way, it reminded me of the day my daughter was born. I'd been imagining and anticipating the moment for so long, but when it actually came, for just a second or two, she seemed like a stranger to me because I'd never actually seen her face.

Same sort of feeling, watching this younger Obi-Wan and his Jedi mentor staring out the windows of the Trade Federation ship in the first few minutes of the movie.

I went into *The Phantom Menace* spoiler-free, but I'd also taken care of a different sort: As giddy as I was, I also made sure I was going into the movie with expectations adjusted. I wasn't six years old anymore, and walking into that theater with the attitude that I was going to have my world rocked the way it had been two-plus decades earlier would have been a sure-fire recipe for disappointment.

I went in expecting fun, and I got it. I got Jedi smacking laser bolts like batting practice, podracing that left my eyeballs drying out in the hot wind, and a three-way lightsaber clash to some of the best John Williams music ever. And when we left the theater that night, I was floating and unable to stop talking about the movie.

(Yes, I also got midichlorians, Jar Jar, poop and fart slapstick, ridiculous plot contrivances, "Yippeeee," a two-headed sportscaster and a horrifically lame space battle, though, as with *Jedi* years before, I didn't really notice the movie's faults at the time.)

Of course, I couldn't say a word about it to Jim, because we were all still planning to go to opening night at Pleasure Island. So for more than a week, the only people I could talk to about the movie were Jenn and Andy and some of my fellow posters in the online *Star Wars* newsgroups.

On the real opening night, then, Jenn and Andy and Jim and I queued up outside the Pleasure Island theaters with a couple thousand other people. We had little paper party-favor *Episode I* masks that hooked over our ears like 3-D glasses. I remember it was odd, being there and having already seen the movie.

Truth is, on just my second viewing, I fought drowsiness in some of those dragging Tatooine scenes, Jar Jar became a little more grating, the midichlorians turned a little more cheesy, and the whole justification for the pod race felt a little more convoluted and goofy.

Digression: When my daughter was two years old, just after *Phantom Menace* came out, someone – I don't remember who, but you can bet it wasn't me – got her some pajamas with a big glow-in-the-dark Jar Jar Binks face on the tummy.

She wore them once, then confessed that she couldn't sleep because Jar Jar's face scared her.

Totally, TOTALLY understandable, kiddo.

Even with its flaws, *Phantom Menace* had its moments, and I still saw it a few more times, including once on a big Imax screen and once in the dollar theaters after Jenn and Kelsey and I had moved up to Ohio that July.

Between *The Phantom Menace* and the 2002 release of *Attack of the Clones*, the *Star Wars* hype tide kind of receded a bit, and it was during this familiar three-year wait, that I finally shared the complete original trilogy with my daughter.

It's especially appropriate at this point, I think, because my wife and daughter and I now live in the same neighborhood where I grew up. I built tree forts in the woods behind the house were we live, and the sun sets across the street behind the same cornfield that's been there since I was six.

Kelsey had been exposed to the movies since before she was born, of course, and I watched them fairly regularly, but it wasn't until she was five – maybe even awfully close to six – that we sat down together intent of watching *Star Wars*.

It was a joy and a struggle.

I loved seeing her get wrapped up in the story and the action and her own concern for the characters. At the same time, I had to fight the urge to point things out or explain them or ask if she understood something or rewind a scene so she could hear some dialogue she'd missed. I didn't do these things, though, because I wanted her to see it the way I had: Young and wide-eyed and even a little confused but still swept away by the scope and the spaceships and the music. At the same time, I knew it'd probably never hit her quite as deep in the gut as it had me, but God, I wanted her to love it.

Of course, she didn't have to go through the whole grow-three-years-while-you-wait-for-the-next-one thing, so she saw *Empire* and *Jedi* through very different eyes than I had.

But she was having fun, and I suddenly had a little *Star Wars* fan on my hands. Maybe not one as intense or toy-focused as I'd been at that age, but one who started coming with me to gatherings of the Ohio *Star Wars* Collectors Club (OSWCC) and coming home with some loot of her own.

Every generation has a legend. Sometimes we're lucky enough to share it with the next one.

Part II: In media res

When the *Attack of the Clones* trailers were released, Kelsey would sit on my lap at the computer, and we'd watch them over and over and over.

When we went to see the re-release of *E.T. – The Extra-Terrestrial*, Kelsey was sitting next to me, and when the *Episode II* preview came onscreen she elbowed me excitedly. She nudged me again during the scene where Elliot was playing with his old *Star Wars* figures.

And although this isn't *Star Wars*-related: We're watching *E.T.*, and it's after they've found the little guy dying in the ditch, and he and

Elliot are getting sicker by the minute. E.T. is lying all crusty and white on the bathroom floor, and I look over at my daughter, and she is weeping hard, but hardly making a sound, these hot tears just pouring down her still-chubby little cheeks. My heart is absolutely shattering. I put my hand on her arm, and she leans in, still sobbing, and says, barely audible: "Daddy…" >sniff!< "Yes, sweetie?" >chokesob!< "E.T. looks like a Frosted Mini-Wheat."

It still makes me almost laugh and cry at the same time.

When the "*Star Wars*: The Magic of Myth" exhibit came to the Toledo Museum of Art in the months before *Episode II* came out, I arranged to cover it for the newspaper where I was working, and Kelsey, Jenn and I made a day trip of it. Seeing my daughter peer at the models and the costumes and props and artwork, I wondered what it was like; what I would have thought at that age, being in a room with the pieces of movie magic under glass right in front of my nose.

I interviewed *Episode I* art director Doug Chiang for about 15 minutes at the exhibit, and he talked to Kelsey before I left. I don't know if she remembers.

She told him she liked Watto. He said he did, too.

In spring 2002, I made a solo one-day road trip to *Star Wars* Celebration II in Indianapolis on a press pass. (I'd actually already paid for an admission badge before realizing that, duh, I was a journalist now and could apply for credentials.)

I hit the road at about 4 or 5 a.m. on a Friday, passed the time listening to The *Star Wars* Radio Drama and a book-on-tape of Philip K. Dick's "The Man in the High Castle" and was in Indianapolis by nine.

In the 24 hours I was there, I went to the opening ceremony emceed by Anthony Daniels, heard prequels producer Rick McCallum talk about the digital filming of *Episode II* – I took notes here for a couple short news features back home – wandered and drooled through the main exhibit hall and the fan fair floor, ate lunch at Steak-n-Shake and dinner at Hooters, ran into Temuera (Jango Fett) Morrison, bought some vintage box flats at one of the room sales that had taken over a floor in the hotel where I was crashing with friends from OSWCC, and saw the extended *Attack of the Clones* preview twice.

The next morning I hit the road again and was home before dinner, as promised, since it was our wedding anniversary and all. (My wife, while not a huge *Star Wars* fan, has always been totally supportive of this sickness I've got, and God, I love her that much more for it.)

I saw *Attack of the Clones* about a week ahead of its release date. The entertainment writer/editor and I sat next to each other in the newsroom, and he asked if I'd want to come see the media screening one morning. (Trick question? Seriously?!?) I figured I could also turn part of this into a movie story using some of those Celebration II notes, which totally justified my taking a chunk out of my workday to go see another *Star Wars* flick.

Excited as I was, this was a totally different atmosphere than the *Phantom Menace* preview: This was specifically a writers' review screening, so there was only a handful of people in the massive stadium-seating theater, and it was all business. Absolutely no buzz, no energy, no excitement in the air. Geeking hard on the inside, I felt wildly out of place and unprofessional, like everyone could see me thinking, "OhmyGodonlyfiveminutesuntilI'mseeingEpisodeII!!!!"

It was almost a distraction, being there and knowing that around me, mental notes were being made at every wince-worthy line of dialogue and every action sequence. I think it made me hyper-aware of the movie's flaws, because when I saw it the next couple times, the parts I had thought were weakest didn't actually seem quite seem so bad.

Jenn and I went opening weekend – though not opening night – because I wanted her to see it before I took Kelsey.

My daughter was five years old when *Attack of the Clones* came out and we saw a matinee with my mom. As I'm working on this essay, Kelsey's eleven, so I asked her what she remembered about that day.

Not much, it turns out. She thinks a little, then: "I remember the guys with the long necks," she says. "They were creepy. The blue guys, who –" and here she goes into a lilting, dreamy voice – "talked all peaaAAAAceful."

Ah, the cloners on Kamino. Anything else?

"I remember thinking it was pretty funny when Yoda started jumping like eight feet in the air."

She didn't remember much about the beginning of the movie, or whether or not she understood what was going on, but she remembered being there with me, and that's really all that needs to be kept for the long haul.

Part III: Closing credits

When the *Episode III: Revenge of the Sith* trailer was released, I had recently resumed my journaling habit, and here's what I wrote on November 9, 2004:

This is the last Star Wars *preview/teaser trailer I will ever get to wait for. Kelsey got off the school bus Thursday, and because I was off work, I met her and said I had a surprise.*

As soon as we sat in front of the computer, she turned around in my lap and said, "Is it a Star Wars *– oh! It's the preview for Episode Three!"*

I hadn't even clicked open the file or given her any hint at all, and I could only break into a huge grin as she kissed me on the cheek.

Either that day or the next, they showed it on MTV's "Total Request Live" – possibly the only thing that could ever get me to watch that show for more than three seconds, unless they sometime decide to bring Martha Quinn back – and I saved the segment on the digital video recorder, watching it pretty much daily and keeping it until after the movie came out months later.

The biggest, best, craziest part of the *Episode III* build-up was the trip Jim and I made to *Star Wars* Celebration III in Indianapolis, just about a month before the movie's May 2005 premiere. We planned this sonofabitch for more than a year and got ourselves a freelance assignment for four days of web coverage and a print feature on the movie.

I had just started a new job, and my first few weeks, Jim and I emailed back and forth constantly, ironing out details about what to cover and how, setting up deadlines, checking the event programming to see who was going to be there and figuring out how to drink it all in. We were seriously, ridiculously psyched.

It was four days of total immersion in *Star Wars* fandom and there's not a second of it I'd give up, even those frustrating times fighting deadlines and cramped media quarters and uncooperative laptops.

Friday evening to Saturday afternoon was particularly packed with "I-can't-believe-we're-here" moments. Starting at about 6 p.m. Friday:

Jim and I met, photographed and interviewed original *Star Wars* model-maker Lorne Peterson. This was a blast. I'd expected, at most, maybe a five-minute chat. We wound up talking for close to half an hour and it was just a very neat thing, thinking that this was a guy who had, quite literally, helped build part of my childhood.

I wound up talking to him a couple more times in the months after C3, and those interviews were the basis for a feature that ran in the October/December 2006 issue of *Filmfax* ("The Magazine of Unusual Film, Television & Retro Pop Culture!"). At 5,000 words, it was easily the longest piece of non-fiction I'd ever written for publication and also my first freelance magazine sale. Seeing it in print accompanied by some ILM-supplied photos and a couple of Jim's shots from C3 was a total adrenaline rush. That these personal milestones were tied to *Star Wars* only makes them that much more meaningful.

On Saturday morning, we woke up at 5 a.m. to secure second-row seats about 25 feet from where George Lucas himself came out for his first fan convention appearance since 1987. Jim shot some amazing photos and got one of George looking *right at us*. He was only onstage maybe 15 minutes, tops, but the whole thing was kind of stunning.

I mean, there he was: this guy whose vision almost 30 years earlier had exploded my imagination's landscape and opened me to seek new ideas and, in ways small and large, seems to have inspired practically every creative thing I've ever done. He was right there, with his gray, wavy hair and his jeans and sweater, sitting on a couch looking a little tired but still smiling.

That night at dinner, we sat under a TV showing a news report from Celebration III, with footage of a kid invited on stage to ask George a question, and we were like, "Wow. We were there." It would happen again over the next few weeks: I'd read an article about *Star Wars* and the saga's end, and there'd be a quote from George Lucas that they'd pulled from his Indianapolis visit, and I'd think, "I was right there when he said that."

We also picked up lunch for Matthew (voice of General Grievous) Wood as a favor to one of the Industrial Light & Magic press contacts who'd been helping us out. Later that night, passing through a large crowd, Matt recognized Jim and me and asked us directions somewhere.

And Saturday afternoon, we were sitting in the mostly-empty press room hanging out with the woman running the place when *Episodes I-III* producer Rick McCallum walked in. (The guy's taken a lot of flack for his role in the prequels and for not being more questioning of George's ideas, but I'll say this: Given Lucas' general avoidance of fan gatherings and public appearances, McCallum made a hell of an impression during the second *Star Wars* era in terms of fan availability and accessibility.)

So McCallum walks in, sees us talking, tosses over a casual, "Hi, guys, how you doing?" and starts talking with one of the Lucasfilm reps. Jim and I play it cool, steering our conversation back on track and somehow managing not to scream like my wife might once have done at a Menudo show.

Now this other press guy starts talking to Rick, and Jim and I had heard that with George Lucas leaving town soon, the Lucasfilm folks would probably be packing up, too, so we went over to the woman McCallum had been talking to so we could thank her for helping us out the past couple days. As we're thanking her, she gets McCallum's attention and introduces us to him.

For the next couple minutes, we were standing there – no pens, no notebooks, no cameras, no recorders, no interview-style questions. It was just three guys talking *Star Wars*, and it was freaking cool as hell.

Revenge of the Sith opened about a month after C3, on May 19th, and I took Kelsey to a 7 p.m. showing.

She was only eight, but she was (and is) a smart, level-headed kid about stuff she reads and watches and listens to. She'd already seen and loved the whole *Lord of the Rings* trilogy, for instance, and given the way *Episodes I* and *II* had played out, I seriously couldn't imagine Lucas putting anything onscreen scarier than Peter Jackson's vision of Tolkien's orcs and ringwraiths, even with *Episode III* getting the PG-13 treatment.

This was also our first and last real chance to share a *Star Wars* opening night together. I'd actually passed up a chance to go see a media screening of *Episode III* because I wanted to be in a crowd of fans with my daughter, both of us experiencing the whole thing for the first time.

I bought tickets online, and on the afternoon of the 19th, I left work a little early so we could have dinner before the movie. It was just Kelsey and me going, since Jenn had to be at work before sunup the next morning.

It was a school night, and I kept thinking about that opening night of *Jedi* back in '83, and I wondered if Kelsey would be as excited the next day at school as I had been, even if she kept it hidden.

I pulled out that old brown bathrobe, put it on over my clothes and threatened to wear it as a Jedi costume, to Kelsey's eye-rolling horror. (I didn't, of course. But even if I had, I wouldn't have been any worse than the guy who showed up at the theater in a *green* bathrobe over a gray hooded sweatshirt. At least, I *hope* his was a goofy costume attempt. Otherwise, that's just weird.) She let me get away with wearing a tiny gold "Star Wars is Forever" pin that I got as a C3 giveaway.

We got to the theater about an hour early, I think. Far enough in advance that they weren't seating yet, so we got to stand in line with other fans for a while. The hardcores, naturally, had seen the movie at the midnight showing, but there was still a smiling kind of thrill running through the crowd. Lots of people my age and a good amount of kids.

A fair amount of teenagers, which kind of surprised me, but at the same time was kind of neat. My youngest brother was a high school teacher then, and he said the kids in his classes were all really pumped about seeing the movie, which he hadn't expected. I mean, I've always thought of the *Star Wars* saga as belonging to "my generation," but now that I think about it, these were the kids who were seven, eight, maybe nine years old when *Phantom Menace* had come out, so they'd grown up on the prequels the way we had on the originals.

So we get our seats and Kelsey and I are looking around and saying we can't believe it's finally here and how great is this and the lights dim and we look at each other and we're both big-eyed and giggly and the previews roll and then BAM that music starts and we are on the ride.

The movie's got its weaknesses, of course, but I remember a couple real heart-in-the-throat and goosebump moments: The wordless scene with the ethereal, tense music that accompanies Anakin and Padmé as they stare separately at the same sunset over the capital city is one of my favorites. And when Anakin and Obi-Wan finally started their lightsaber duel, I felt my muscles and my stomach clench like the moment you go over that first great drop on a rollercoaster, because this was *it*, man, this was the fight all us first-generation fans had wondered about for so long. (Funny thing: I only recently stopped to consider that this battle isn't even really mentioned onscreen in the original trilogy – it's only in the *Jedi* novelization that Obi-Wan actually describes his first duel with Vader.)

In between, there's the scene where Anakin returns to the Jedi temple to start his rampage. This was the part I was a little worried about, because a month earlier, at C3, in the hours spent waiting to see George Lucas, I overheard this snippet of conversation: "…even kills the kids…" I tried my best to block it out, but you can't unhear something, and even though I told myself that just because I'd heard it didn't make it true – 12 *Star Wars* movies all shown in Kansas, remember? Darth Vader funhouse, anyone? – I still couldn't help but wonder if I'd made a mistake bringing my 8-year-old daughter.

At this point in the movie, right after Anakin goes bad, Kelsey is literally on the edge of her seat. I cast a glance her way when Anakin goes into the room with the younglings. She's got her hands folded tightly in her lap, and she isn't blinking and she is actually whispering barely above a breath, "Don't do it, don't do it, no, no, no…"

My throat catches and I'm barely breathing, because, like me on *Jedi's* opening night, she is *there*, she is *in that room* and living the story. For just a moment, I'm excited for her and maybe even a little envious.

After the movie ended – and that double-sunset scene and its musical score was the perfect conclusion and throwback – Kelsey and I let out deep breaths and smiled. We talked a lot in the car on the way home, me turning my head slightly to carry on a conversation with her in the backseat because she couldn't ride up front yet. It was late and we had work and school early in the morning, and we were both tired but still a little keyed up.

The short drive captured everything I love about *Star Wars*: After 30 years, it's more about the shared experience and energy and excitement of that universe than anything that can be confined to a movie frame.

Times like that are why you'll never hear me wish George Lucas hadn't made the prequels.

So I got stuck with midichlorians.

Small price to pay.

Acknowledgments

For as much as these are my memories and stories, this book collecting them simply doesn't happen without the support and guidance and just plain friendship of an awful lot of people.

At the top of that list are my wife Jennifer and my daughter Kelsey, who love and encourage me beyond measure, tolerating and even managing to embrace this whole *Star Wars* obsession. They also know when to tell me to get off the computer already and come play Guitar Hero because I need a butt-kicking.

Adam Besenyodi, my longtime friend and, in recent years, editor, regularly downplayed his contributions during the umpteen revisions of my work. He's way too modest. In addition to the nuts-and-bolts copyediting he did, Adam constantly pulled better writing out of me, and his fingerprints are all over this book.

Jim Carchidi is my constant fellow *Star Wars* nutcase adventurer, co-founder of FieldsEdge.com, photographer extraordinaire, and the guy who throws jars of gasoline on every geek project spark that comes out of my head. His enthusiasm leaves point-five past lightspeed in the dust.

My mom, Pam Booth Caldwell, and my dad, the late Rich Booth, gave me a childhood well worth keeping and a life's worth of lessons in doing the same down the road. And a lot of *Star Wars* toys, too.

Nicholas Booth and Adam Booth pulled the coolest role-reversal ever in handing down their *Star Wars* stuff to their older brother for safekeeping.

And in no particular order, thanks to the many others who shared these memories, created these moments, and encouraged my fandom and writing: Michael Smit, Mike Darrow, Jacob Maurer, Aaron Archer, Ivan Knapp, Mindé Briscoe, Robert Schoenberger, Lorne Peterson, Mark Corcoran, Renita Jablonski, Trevor Porter, Tracy Besenyodi, Keith Marsteller, the entire Ohio Star Wars Collectors Club and the crew roaming the vintage forum halls of Rebelscum.com.

Finally, thanks to George Lucas, the Maker.

Bring on parts seven through twelve.

John Booth
June, 2008

About the author

If you've read this far, you pretty much know where John lives, where he grew up, and that he's a wee bit of a *Star Wars* fan. He's also an award-winning journalist, a 1980s pop culture dork, a casual runner, a brachiopod hunter, and the author of the novel *Crossing Decembers*.

CPSIA information can be obtained at www.ICGtesting.com
Printed in the USA
LVOW05s1555011013

354945LV00003B/697/P